The Family Handbook

by Katie Duckworth
and Charlotte Sankey

THE NATIONAL TRUST

Written by Charlotte Sankey and Katie Duckworth
for Loudmouth Communications, Cambridge

Illustrations by Tiffany Sharp

Published in Great Britain in 2000
by National Trust (Enterprises) Ltd,
36 Queen Anne's Gate, London SW1H 9AS

http://www.bookshelf.nationaltrust.org.uk
ISBN 0 7078 0321 7

Designed by Charlotte Sankey for
Loudmouth Communications, Cambridge

Printed by Wing King Tong Co. Ltd.

Contents

Introduction 4

    How to use this book 6

    Symbols 10

    More about your visit 11

    National Trust contacts 13

    Map 14

The properties by region

    South West 16

    South and South East 45

    London 71

    East 75

    Central 93

    North West 108

    North East 120

    Wales 144

    Northern Ireland 156

Index of properties by name 166

Photographic credits 168

Introduction

Why does *The Family Handbook* stand out from other
National Trust guides? It looks at 125 Trust properties from
a quite different perspective: through a child's eyes.
Whatever is on offer – historic houses, castles, gardens or
beautiful stretches of coast and countryside – your family
will be sure to find all kinds of things to see and do at
the properties included here, and you'll be assured of a
warm welcome.

This book is bursting with wonderful places to go, where
the kids can channel their energy into romping around
beautiful parklands, gazing at weird and wonderful
treasures in some of the most stunning houses in the
world, or having a go at discovery and nature trails.

The places included are particularly suitable for families for
one or more of the following reasons:
  ● there are good family-friendly facilities

- the property itself is of particular interest to children
- there are plenty of things to do, such as quiz sheets and trails
- frequent family events or children's activities take place
- there are wide open spaces to play and walk in.

You never know what interest you might awaken in your children with a visit to National Trust properties: birds, insects, farm animals, statues, dolls' houses, mazes, mills, mines, children's lives in past times.... Or they may simply have an invigorating day out which will leave you feeling refreshed. Best of all, if you're members, it's almost all free.

Who is it for?

The Family Handbook will be invaluable for anyone who has children to entertain – parents, grandparents, uncles and aunts, friends. The text has been written for adults but is lively enough to be read by older children. The fold-out quiz pages and stickers are for children of any age to entertain themselves at the property, or on the way home.

How to use this book

If you know the name of the property you want to visit, look it up in the index. If you want a property in a particular area, the map on pages 14 and 15 shows you which properties are in which region. Entries are listed in alphabetical order within regions. Each entry follows the same format:

Property title and key words
At a glance these indicate what you will find at each property, eg castle, park, etc. The key words, together with the first paragraph in each entry (which gives a very brief summary of the property and what is of particular interest), should help you to decide fairly quickly whether what's on offer will meet your needs.

Directions and transport
Brief directions give you an idea of where a property is

located. Bus and train directions are also included so that you can 'go green' and leave the car behind. There is more detailed information on directions and other details such as opening times in the companion to this guide, *The National Trust Handbook*. This is available free to members, or for sale in National Trust shops and bookshops.

Price

The only information given under this section is whether a family ticket is available. Prices change each year, so check the current *National Trust Handbook* for the latest details. A family ticket usually allows two adults and up to three children to visit all sections of a property (eg house, garden, museum, etc.) for a set price. Costs do vary considerably, and currently range between £4.50 and £20.00. If the words 'family ticket' do not appear, this means they are not available at that particular property. **Please note:** children under 5 are free and children aged 5–16 are half price.

Membership

Entry for National Trust Members is free to most properties. There are three annual membership categories of interest to families:

- Family membership (two adults living at one address and children or grandchildren under 18)
- Family one adult membership (one adult and children under 18)
- Child membership (individual membership for children under 13)

The Trust also offers family joint life membership (two adults living at one address, and children or grandchildren under 18). For more information about joining the National Trust, contact the membership department on 020 8315 1111.

Introduction

What can you see?

As well as drawing attention to fabulous views and features, this section includes things to look for which may be of particular interest to children. They often highlight quirky things such as secret priest's holes and gruesome creatures carved into woodwork, which are not always what the place is best known for.

What can you do?

This gives suggestions for what children and families can do at each property – again, often including features such as grassy slopes to run down – that the adult literature will not mention. This section also includes activities especially designed for children. These take place usually, but not exclusively, in the school holidays and range from butter-making in the Tudor kitchen at Buckland Abbey to pond dipping at Wicken Fen. There is sometimes a very small extra charge for these activities which are run as part of the Trust's commitment to informal education. Contact individual properties for up-to-date details of activities.

Special events

Entries under this heading tend to include larger, one-off events such as a teddy bears' picnic at Castle Ward or the Apple days at Acorn Bank. There will often be a charge for entry and any one event can attract thousands of families. Events are mainly held in the summer holidays but many properties run Hallowe'en and Christmas events and Easter egg hunts. Events will, of course, change every year and those included for each entry are a taster only. Please contact individual properties for this information, or a free 'Children Welcome' pack, which includes details of all Trust family events, is available on 020 8315 1111. You can also check the Trust's websites (see pages 11 and 12).

By the way...

This section includes any extra information which families may find particularly useful, such as odd opening times, any potential dangers to children or the availability of lavatories.

Symbols

 Playground or play area

 Picnic area

 Animals. This means children can see wild or other animals while on a visit. For instance, this symbol is shown for Wimpole Home Farm. It is also included if there are significant numbers of animals such as squirrels, deer or sheep in parkland around houses, or on other parts of a property.

 Quiz sheet, trail sheet or children's guide. Many properties have fun quiz sheets, trails or guidebooks especially written for children. These cost from just 25p to £2.00-3.00 at ticket points or in National Trust shops at individual properties. Some are free. They are generally written in a child-friendly style and will greatly enhance a child's experience of a property.

 Café or restaurant

   Children's menu. Toys in restaurant. High chair in restaurant. These three symbols relate to practical provision for families in the café or restaurant. Where toys are indicated, these range from Trusty colouring sheets through to robust table-top toys. Bottle warming can be arranged on request. The National Trust is constantly aiming to improve in this area and most properties now offer children's menus and high chairs.

 Wheelchair access. This symbol indicates that a reasonable amount of the property can be enjoyed from a wheelchair without undue difficulty. Outside, wheelchair-friendly areas are likely to be suitable for pushchairs too; for instance, where boardwalks or paths are smooth and flat. Please see below for restrictions on pushchairs.

 Shop

 Dogs on leads in park or garden. Except for guide dogs and hearing dogs, dogs are not allowed into Trust houses, restaurants and gardens. This symbol means dogs are allowed on a lead in parkland. In countryside areas it is advisable to keep your dog on a lead because of the potential danger to animals and other wildlife. Signs at the property will advise whether this is necessary.

 No dogs. A few properties do not allow dogs at all.

 Baby changing and feeding facilities. This symbol indicates that there are facilities for baby changing and feeding, often in a purpose-designed parent and baby room.

 Front-carrying baby slings for loan. Baby back carriers cannot usually be admitted to houses because of the danger of accidental damage. This symbol indicates whether front slings are available for loan as a substitute. Babies carried in front slings are obviously very welcome.

More about your visit

Trusty the Hedgehog

Child members of the National Trust and children visiting properties are likely to come across Trusty the Hedgehog. As a costumed character, Trusty makes frequent appearances at family events where he helps inform children about the Trust's conservation work. Being a modern kind of a hedgehog, he has his own website (www.trusty.org) where  children can contact him by e-mail. He also stars in the children's magazine *Trust Tracks* which is available free to child members under 13. A range of Trusty merchandise is available in National Trust shops, and restaurants often have Trusty tuck boxes or other Trusty-inspired goodies.

NT Education

As well as running a full programme of informal education and events, the Trust has a large formal education programme for all ages. For full details please contact the membership department on 020 8315 1111, or access the Education website on www.nationaltrust.org.uk/education.

Touching!

The Trust is very sympathetic to the fact that children want to touch furniture and objects since they are bound to be excited and intrigued by what they are seeing. Unfortunately, in the majority of historic houses, we must ask you to explain to children that they should not do so. Even clean hands leave marks which can damage furniture, fabrics and other precious items. Although it may seem harsh, this is the only way that houses and their contents can be preserved for future visitors.

There are some properties where visitors may touch items, such as at Washington Old Hall. Increasingly, property staff have put together 'handling collections' of objects such as

kitchen utensils. In some properties there are items which
visually impaired visitors are invited to touch. Individual
entries highlight these opportunities.

Pushchairs

Please note that unlike wheelchairs, pushchairs are not
generally allowed inside historic houses. This is because of
the risk of accidents to babies and young children, and to
protect delicate contents from being damaged unintentionally.
At some properties, entry is at the discretion of the Property
Manager so it's always worth checking. On quiet weekdays,
for instance, it may be possible to bring pushchairs into a
house, at least to the ground floor.

Thank you

We know that some of the restrictions necessary at
properties can be difficult for families. Please be assured
that they have been introduced only after much research
and thought. The Trust faces major challenges in preserving
houses which were not designed for large numbers of
visitors, but for living in. Thank you for your understanding
and acceptance of the reasons behind these measures.

Publications

The National Trust publishes *Investigating* ..., a series of
paperbacks that are ideal for 7–13 year olds. With their line
drawings and photographs, they bring to life dramatic
periods of history using Trust properties as a focus. Priced
at £3.99, they can be bought in National Trust shops and
in general bookshops, or you can order them through our
website: **http://www.bookshelf.nationaltrust.org.uk**
Titles currently available: *The Romans*, *Medieval Times*,
The Tudors, *The Civil War*, *The Eighteenth Century*, *The
Victorians*, *The Home Front*, *Childhood*, *Food in History*,
Gardens, *Family History*, *Design*, *Myths & Legends*.

National Trust contacts

1. **National Trust Membership Department**, PO Box 39, Bromley, Kent BR1 3XL
   (tel. 020 8315 1111; fax. 020 8466 6824; email enquiries@ntrust.org.uk) for all general enquiries, including membership and requests for literature
2. **London Head Office**, 36 Queen Anne's Gate, London SW1H 9AS
   (tel. 020 7222 9251; fax. 020 7222 5097). National Trust guidebooks can be purchased from the reception desk
3. **National Trust Regional Offices in England**
   Cornwall: Lanhydrock, Bodmin PL30 4DE (tel. 01208 74281; fax. 01208 77887)
   Devon: Killerton House, Broadclyst, Exeter EX5 3LE
   (tel. 01392 881691; fax. 01392 881954)
   East Anglia (*Cambridgeshire, Essex, Norfolk & Suffolk*): Blickling, Norwich NR11 6NF (tel. 01263 733471; fax. 01263 734924)
   East Midlands (*Derbyshire, Leicestershire, Lincolnshire, Northamptonshire, Nottinghamshire & all of the Peak District*): Clumber Park Stableyard, Worksop, Notts S80 3BE
   (tel. 01909 486411; fax. 01909 486377)
   Kent & East Sussex (*including SE London*): The Estate Office, Scotney Castle, Lamberhurst, Tunbridge Wells, Kent TN3 8JN
   (tel. 01892 890651; fax. 01892 890110)
   Mercia (*Cheshire, Manchester, Merseyside, Shropshire & Staffordshire*): Attingham Park, Shrewsbury, Shropshire SY4 4TP
   (tel. 01743 708100; fax. 01743 708150)
   North West (*Cumbria & Lancashire*): The Hollens, Grasmere, Ambleside, Cumbria LA22 9QZ
   (tel. 015394 35599; fax. 015394 35353)
   Northumbria (*Durham, Northumberland, Newcastle & Tyneside*):
   Scots' Gap, Morpeth, Northumberland NE61 4EG
   (tel. 01670 774691; fax. 01670 774317)
   Severn (*Gloucestershire, Herefordshire, Warwickshire, West Midlands & Worcestershire*): Mythe End House, Tewkesbury, Glos GL20 6EB
   (tel. 01684 850051; fax. 01684 850090)
   Southern (*Hampshire, Isle of Wight, SW London, Surrey & West Sussex*): Polesden Lacey, Dorking, Surrey RH5 6BD
   (tel. 01372 453401; fax. 01372 452023)
   Thames & Chilterns (*Bedfordshire, Berkshire, Buckinghamshire, Hertfordshire, N London & Oxfordshire*): Hughenden Manor, High Wycombe, Bucks HP14 4LA (tel. 01494 528051; fax. 01494 463310)
   Wessex (*Bristol/Bath, Dorset, Somerset & Wiltshire*):
   Eastleigh Court, Bishopstrow, Warminster, Wiltshire BA12 9HW
   (tel. 01985 843600; fax. 01985 843624)
   Yorkshire (*including Teesside*): Goddards, 27 Tadcaster Road, Dringhouses, York YO24 1GG (tel. 01904 702021; fax. 01904 771970)
4. **National Trust Office for Wales**
   Trinity Square, Llandudno, Gwynedd LL30 2DE
   (tel. 01492 860123; fax. 01492 860233)
5. **National Trust Office for Northern Ireland**
   Rowallane House, Saintfield, Ballynahinch, Co. Down BT24 7LH
   (tel. 01238 510721; fax. 01238 511242)
6. **Volunteers Office**, 33 Sheep St, Cirencester, Glos GL7 1RQ
   (tel. 01285 651818), or contact the Regional Volunteers Coordinator in each region (see list of Regional Offices above) for details of volunteer opportunities
7. **National Trust Enterprises**, The Stable Block, Heywood House, Westbury, Wilts BA13 4NA
   (tel. 01373 858787) for matters relating to shops, restaurants, holidays and the gift catalogue. For **Mail Order**, write to PO Box 101, Melksham, Wiltshire SN12 8EA (tel. 01225 790800); for **Holiday Cottage** information, tel. 01225 791199
8. **National Trust Theatre Projects**, The National Trust, Sutton House,
   2 & 4 Homerton High Street, Hackney, London E9 6JQ (tel. 020 8986 0242)

Introduction

Map

South West
1 Arlington Court
2 Avebury
3 Brownsea Island
4 Buckland Abbey
5 Castle Drogo
6 Corfe Castle
7 Cornish Mines & Engines
8 Cotehele House & Quay
9 Dunster Castle
10 Dyrham Park
11 Finch Foundry
12 Glendurgan Garden
13 Killerton House
14 Lacock Abbey
15 Lanhydrock
16 Lydford Gorge
17 Overbecks
18 St Michael's Mount
19 Stourhead
20 Studland Beach
21 Trelissick
22 Trerice

South & South East
23 Ashridge Estate
24 Basildon Park
25 Bateman's
26 Bodiam Castle
27 Box Hill
28 Claremont Landscape Garden
29 Claydon House
30 Dapdune Wharf & Navigations
31 Devil's Dyke
32 Gateway to the White Cliffs & South Foreland Lighthouse
33 Greys Court
34 Hughenden Manor
35 Ightham Mote
36 Needles Old Battery
37 Nymans Gardens
38 Petworth House
39 Polesden Lacey
40 Sheffield Park Garden
41 Stowe Landscape Gardens
42 Witley and Milford Commons

London
43 Morden Hall Park & Snuff Mill
44 Osterley Park
45 Sutton House

East
46 Anglesey Abbey
47 Belton House
48 Blickling Hall
49 Dunwich Heath & Minsmere Beach
50 Felbrigg Hall
51 Hatfield Forest
52 Houghton Mill
53 Ickworth House and Park
54 Oxburgh Hall
55 Tattershall Castle
56 Wicken Fen
57 Wimpole Home Farm
58 Woolsthorpe Manor

Central
59 Baddesley Clinton
60 Berrington Hall
61 Canons Ashby House
62 Calke Abbey
63 Carding Mill Valley
64 Charlecote Park
65 Chedworth Roman Villa
66 Clumber Park
67 Ilam Park
68 Kedleston Hall
69 Mr Straw's House
70 Snowshill Manor
71 Sudbury Hall & Museum of Childhood

North West
72 Acorn Bank
73 Fell Foot Park
74 Formby
75 Gawthorpe Hall
76 Little Moreton Hall
77 Lyme Park
78 Rufford Old Hall
79 Sizergh Castle
80 Speke Hall
81 Townend

North East
82 Beningbrough Hall
83 Brimham Rocks
84 Cragside
85 Cherryburn
86 East Riddlesden Hall
87 Farne Islands
88 Fountains Abbey & Studley Royal
89 Gibside
90 George Stephenson's Birthplace
91 Hadrian's Wall & Housesteads Fort
92 Hardcastle Crags
93 Lindisfarne Castle
94 Nostell Priory
95 Nunnington Hall
96 Ormesby Hall
97 Souter Lighthouse
98 Treasurer's House
99 Washington Old Hall
100 Wallington

Wales
101 Chirk Castle
102 Colby Woodland Garden
103 Dinefwr Park
104 Dolaucothi Gold Mines
105 Erddig
106 Penrhyn Castle
107 Plas Newydd
108 Powis Castle

Northern Ireland
109 Ardress House
110 The Argory
111 Castle Ward & Strangford Lough
112 Crom Estate
113 Florence Court
114 Giant's Causeway
115 Mount Stewart
116 Springhill & Wellbrook Beetling Mill

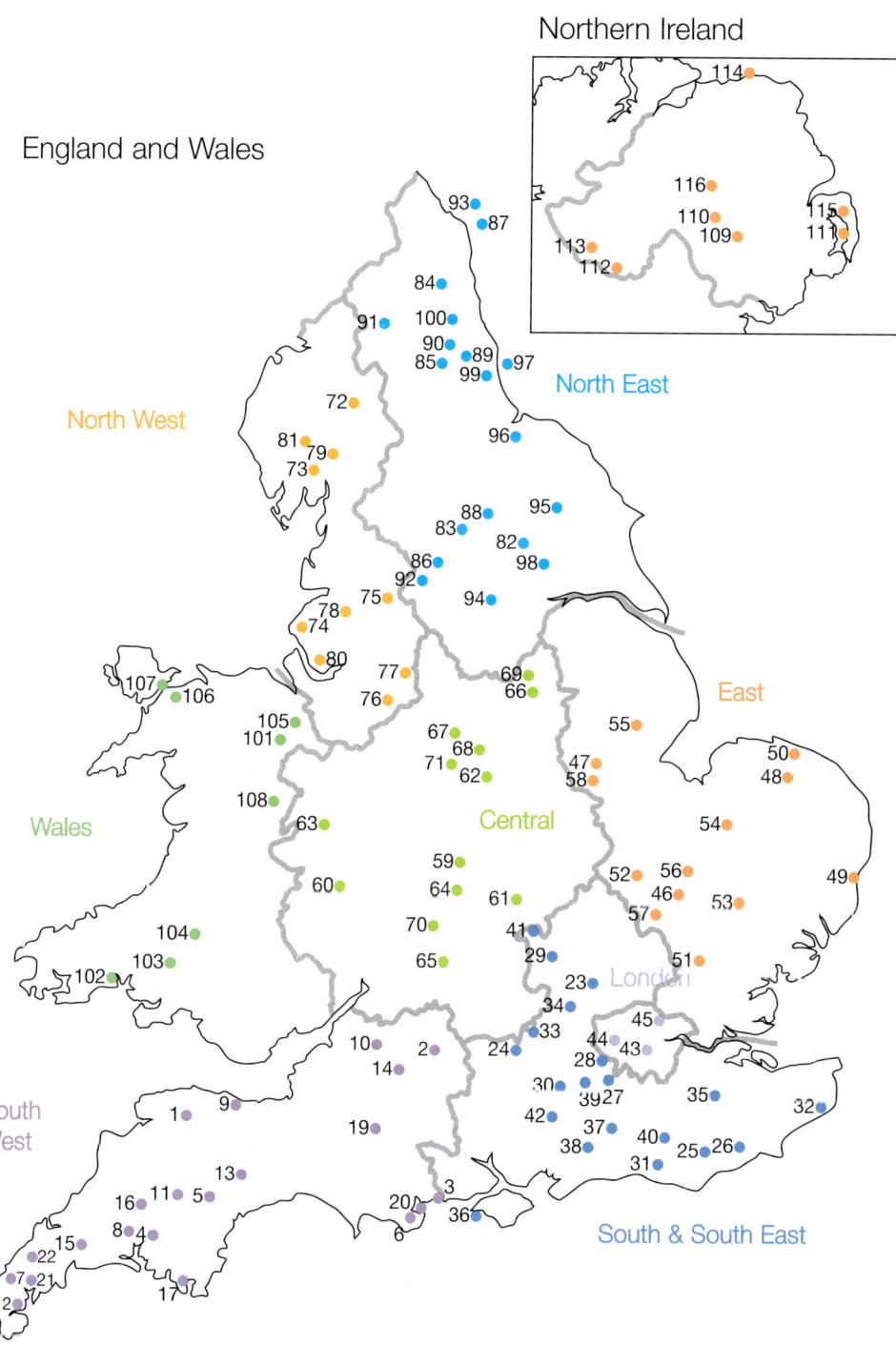

Northern Ireland

England and Wales

North West

North East

East

Wales

Central

London

South West

South & South East

Introduction

Arlington Court

Historic house Museum Lake Park Woods

Arlington, nr Barnstaple,
Devon EX31 4LP
Tel (01271) 850296

7ml NE Barnstaple on
A39. Barnstaple station
8ml. Bus: Red Bus 309.

Family ticket

Arlington Court was once the home of eccentric collector, Rosalie Chichester. She was a great traveller and her house is overflowing with fascinating objects from the countries she visited. Children love Arlington's wiry Jacob sheep and Shetland ponies and playing on their own carriage in the Carriage Museum.

Animal antics

Miss Chichester adored animals. She had three peacocks called Spangles, Sapphire and Speckles who used to wander the house freely. The ponies and sheep that live here today are descended from ones she brought back from Australia and New Zealand.

What can you see?

- Cabinets of stuffed birds and seashells, silver spoons and model ships. In the nursery there's a Victorian trapeze artist in a glass case and a clockwork tortoise.
- In the Carriage Museum there are nearly 50 horse-drawn carriages and a carriage designed to be pulled by a dog.

What can you do?

- Take hold of the reins and 'drive' the 'please touch' carriage in the carriage collection – the metal horse won't take you far, though.
- Go for a trot round the estate with a little help from the real-life carriage horses.

By the way...

Arlington is not open on Saturdays, except bank holiday weekends.

This Chinese red amber elephant can be seen in the White Drawing Room.

Avebury

Ancient monument   Museum   Walks

The standing stones at Avebury are one of the most important megalithic monuments in Europe. They're an awesome sight and will provoke scores of unanswerable questions. Avebury is one of 440 World Heritage Sites along with the Taj Mahal and the Pyramids. Don't miss it.

Nr Marlborough, Wiltshire SN8 1RF
Tel (01672) 539250

6ml W of Marlborough, 1ml N of A4 on A4361 and B4003. Swindon station 11ml. Bus: Thamesdown 49A, Wilts & Dorset 5/6.

Get dug in

The massive ditch around the stones was dug with picks made of antlers, and shovels made from the shoulder blades of oxen.

What can you see?

- The huge stones, arranged in circles c. 2500BC.
- One of the longest burial mounds (or barrows) in England and Wales.
- The Barber Surgeon's Stone under which the remains of a medieval man were discovered in 1938 with scissors in his pocket – hence the name.

What can you do?

- Marvel at how and why the stones got here – it's still a mystery.
- Visit the Alexander Keiller Museum to find out what is known about Avebury's history.
- Buy the lively children's guide to help children think about what they're seeing.
- Walk up the stone-lined West Kennet Avenue and imagine life in prehistoric times.

By the way...

It's free to visit the stones and a small fee to go to the museum.

Brownsea Island

Countryside Harbour Walks

Poole Harbour, Dorset
BH13 7EE
Tel (01202) 707744

In Poole Harbour.
Poole station $1/2$ ml to
quay. Boat to the Island.
Bus: Wilts & Dorset
150/152, Yellow Buses
12 and 30.

Family ticket

Smugglers' heaven

Brownsea Island was the
perfect haunt for smugglers
who used to hide their booty
of silks and spices in the
castle here. In the 19th
century twenty coastguards
worked round the clock to put
a stop to the smuggling – not
very successfully!

What can you see?

- Red squirrels in the tall pine
  woods. Brownsea is one of
  only two remaining habitats
  for these in the south of
  Britain. The other is the Isle
  of Wight.
- All sorts of sea birds such as
  oyster-catchers and terns
  which you'll spot nose-div-
  ing into the sea.
- Lots of proud peacocks.
- The ruins of the 19th-
  century brickworks, now
  protected from tumbling
  into the sea, and the
  pottery workers' cottages.

What can you do?

- Take the boat to Brownsea
  from Poole Quay, Swanage,
  Bournemouth or Sandbacks.
  See local information for
  fares and timetable.
- Follow the smugglers' trail
  to the treasure chest by
  finding letters of the

*A Canada goose
keeps its eggs
warm on the
shingle shore of
Brownsea Island.*

alphabet on posts around the island. It takes about an hour and children can then claim their certificate and Trusty sticker.

- Similar leaflets, including the explorers' and historical trails, are available at the quay.
- Pack your picnic or enjoy a Trusty tuck box from the café.
- In the summer go for a guided walk in the nature reserve which is not usually open to the public. Contact the Dorset Wildlife Trust warden on (01202) 709445.

Special events

Every year there's an Easter Sunday trail on a different theme and fun family events are held throughout the year.

By the way...

- Take your little one around the island in one of eight all-terrain baby buggies available free from the reception on the quay.

Brownsea Island is one of only two remaining habitats for red squirrels in the south of Britain.

There are two larger buggies for older children with restricted mobility.

- Sorry, you'll have to leave the dog behind. They are not allowed on the island because of the wildlife.

Buckland Abbey

Historic house Walks

Yelverton, Devon
PL20 6EY
Tel (01822) 853607

6ml S of Tavistock; 11ml
N of Plymouth off A386.
Plymouth station 11ml.
Bus: Plymouth Citybus
55 from Yelverton.

Family ticket

There's so much going on here that it's a shame to visit Buckland Abbey without children. They'll want to find out about its famous owner, Sir Francis Drake, but don't forget to look for reminders of the original 13th-century abbey, once home to Cistercian monks.

Bowled over

Sir Francis Drake is famous for his sea voyage around the world and his defeat of the Spanish Armada. He was also great friends with Queen Elizabeth I. There is a well-known story that he was enjoying an exciting game of bowls one day in 1588, so that when the ships of the Armada sailed into view, he calmly carried on with his game. Luckily he won (the battle, not the game), otherwise he and the Queen might not have stayed quite so friendly – she had a fearsome temper!

What can you see?

- In the Drake Chamber the perfect new ceiling made with yak hair plaster. The original went up in flames.
- The kitchen, full of clues to 400 years of history.
- The 'magic' drum in the Pym Gallery. It's said that if ever England is in danger the drum should be beaten and Drake will come back from the dead.
- Old doorways and windows which were part of the original abbey.
- Traditional craft workers in the ox sheds.

What can you do?

- In the school holidays and on bank holidays the Abbey is bursting with activity.

- Have a go at butter-making or old-fashioned tub laundry.
- Play Armada noughts and crosses in the Pym Gallery.
- Meet the great man himself as he walks about his home (or is it his ghost...?).
- Get a good sniff of the 40 different herbs in the herb garden – grown for medicines as well as for cooking.

Special events

Buckland Abbey has a very impressive programme of family events and activities. Recent events have included Drake activity days, bug hunts and a Tudor trail to search for missing treasure and, of course, games of bowls. The 'Kidstuff' leaflet outlines it all and is available by ringing the number above.

By the way...

Children should be accompanied by an adult to all events (and, unfortunately for youthful grown-ups, vice versa).

Castle Drogo

Historic house   Garden   Walks

Drewsteignton, nr Exeter,
Devon EX6 6PB
Tel (01647) 433306

5ml S of A30
Exeter–Okehampton road
via Crockernwell.
Yeoford station 8ml.
Bus: Carmel 174 from
Okehampton; DevonBus
173 from Exeter.

Family ticket

Just the name conjures up somewhere extraordinary, and your family certainly won't be disappointed when they get to Castle Drogo. It sits high on a rocky outcrop above the River Teign with dramatic views over Dartmoor. Designed by the famous architect Edwin Lutyens, the 'castle' was built between 1910 and 1932. He must have had fun planning it – the outside looked like an imposing medieval castle, but inside it was a modern, comfortable family home.

Super rich

The first owner, Julius Drewe, became a millionaire when he was only 33 through his chain of grocery shops, the Home and Colonial Stores. Wanting an ancient ancestry, he 'discovered' that he was descended from an important Norman baron called Drogo de Teign – hence the name of the castle.

The Bunty House.

What can you see?

- Look out for all the fake medieval details such as the portcullis, 2-metre (6-foot) thick walls, and turrets with arrow slits.
- A lion carved into the entrance tower, and similar ones all over the castle. The lion was the family's emblem.
- The mini table-football used for tournaments by the

Drewe children, Adrian, Basil and Cedric.

- The kitchens and other rooms 'below stairs' designed by Lutyens – he even planned the huge plate racks and giant pestle and mortar.
- A fabulous old-fashioned bath and weighing scales.
- The Bunty House in the cottage garden, where Julius's grandchildren played in the summer.

What can you do?

- Follow the children's guidebook to learn more about the castle as you explore.
- Look out for the lift and telephone – in their day, the latest in labour-saving devices.
- Walk down the servants' staircase – they had a separate one so that the family wouldn't have to bump into them.
- Play croquet on the lawn. You can hire a set at the visitor reception.
- Take a walk from the castle to the dramatic Teign Gorge. Pick up a leaflet outlining this and other walks at the shop.

Special events

Recent summer events for families have included wildlife walks, face painting and a treasure hunt. In addition there are usually children's activities going on in the summer half-term. Check for details.

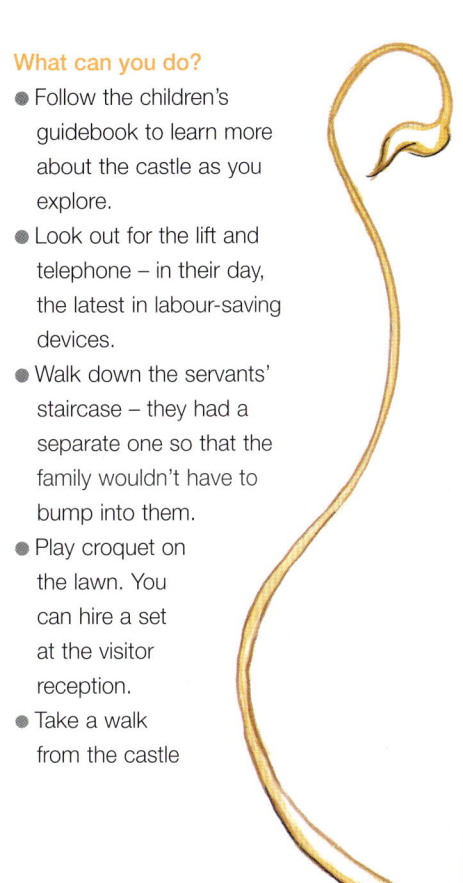

By the way...

Babies are very welcome to enjoy a visit to Castle Drogo in their back carrier.

Corfe Castle

Ruins   Visitor centre

Corfe Castle, Wareham,
Dorset BH20 5EZ
Tel (01929) 481294

On A351
Wareham–Swanage road.
Corfe Castle station is a
few minutes' walk.
Steam railway from
Swanage to Norden Park
& Ride.

Family ticket

If you're holidaying in the area, let your imaginations run riot at this romantic ruined castle with its spectacular views over Poole Harbour. Follow Trusty the Hedgehog on his Corfe Castle Trail and press all kinds of knobs and buttons in an interactive display in the visitor centre. In the Easter, half-term and summer holidays children can join in with a whole range of extra free activities which don't need to be booked.

Bloody history

Corfe Castle was built by William the Conqueror in the 11th century and left in ruins by the Parliamentarians 600 years later. Its history is full of violence and murder. Twenty-two knights starved to death in its grisly dungeons on the orders of wicked King John.

What can you see?

- The evocative remains of its thick walls, fireplaces, stairways and even the old lavatories make it easy to imagine medieval life here.
- Spot the 'murder holes' in the gatehouse through which soldiers flung stones and boiling water (in fact, pretty much anything they could lay their hands on).

What can you do?

- Try out the hands-on display in the visitor centre.
- Find out who was the first English king to wear a dressing gown, and what Lady Bankes thought of the lavatories.
- You may be lucky and find that the Study Room is open when you visit. If so, children can parade about in early medieval and Civil War outfits, and examine the archaeological finds discovered here.
- Go for a walk on nearby Corfe Common or visit the pretty village, also called Corfe Castle (the game of football – with a blown-up pig's bladder – may have been invented here).

Special events

Corfe runs lots of exciting events such as hands-on archaeological weekends in September. Each May the English Civil War Society holds dramatic re-enactments of the famous 1643 siege of the castle by Cromwell's Roundheads.

By the way...

- The Study Room at Castle View Visitor Centre is open most days through the summer holidays. To avoid disappointment, please check in advance what's on.
- **Please note:** under 17s must be accompanied in the castle.

Cannonballs, grapeshot and lead, dating from the Civil War, dug up at Corfe Castle.

Cornish Coast

Cornwall has some of the most stunning scenery in the UK: secluded coves, craggy cliffs, sandy beaches and wooded valleys which can all be reached by a network of footpaths.

Top and right: The beach at Crackington Haven has something for everyone.

Crackington Haven

6ml NE of Boscastle, 8ml SW of Bude

Crackington Haven is a heavenly family beach (not NT). It has great rock pools, waves for body boarding, an excellent café and plenty of flat sand at low tide. On either side are dramatic walks along the NT cliffs, with the famous 'Crackington formation' in the rocks. At Trevigue, a slate-roofed farmhouse a mile up the coast, you can go on badger watches and other nature walks with the tenant (tel 01840 230418 for details). The NT also looks after nearby 'High Cliff', the highest cliff in Cornwall, with fine views.

Boscastle

$3^1/_2$ ml NE of Tintagel on B3263 Bude road

On Cornwall's north coast, Boscastle is an old fishing village with an unusual harbour. It makes a dramatic starting point for a coastal walk (quite steep, so better for older children). If you walk out far enough at certain tides, you can see where the sea gets dramatically sprayed through a blowhole when it meets the first breakwater. There is a National Trust shop in the former blacksmith's forge in the harbour and an information centre in the main car park.

Fowey

The NT owns a number of stretches of countryside around the historic harbour of Fowey at the end of the A3082

A good day's outing is the 4-mile trip around the charming town of Fowey (pronounced 'foy') called the Hall Walk. Catch the Bodinnick car ferry and enjoy the views of the town's busy port. You end up at the little village of Polruan where you can catch another ferry back to Fowey.

Kynance Cove and Lizard Point

SE of Helston off A3294 and 3ml S of Falmouth

Lizard Point, the southernmost point of mainland Britain, was bought through the Enterprise Neptune Appeal. It is a stunning place to wander around. Just west of Lizard Town is the picturesque Kynance Cove which has lovely swimming in clear turquoise waters. There are plenty of good waymarked walks, too.

Cliff walks

There are excellent walks all along Cornwall's coastal path. Particularly breathtaking views can be had at Zennor Head, St Anthony's Head, High Cliff, Rosemergy and Trerean cliffs, and Pentire Head. Keep children a long way back from the edge and dogs on a lead.

Cornish Mines & Engines & Industrial Heritage Centre

Mine Visitor centre

Pool, nr Redruth,
Cornwall
Tel (01209) 315027

At Pool, 2ml W of
Redruth, on either side
of A3047. Redruth and
Camborne stations
both 2ml.

Family ticket

The disused mines dotted across Cornwall's landscape make a dramatic site. Here you have the chance to see what it's like inside – and watch a huge engine in action. Hear also about the lives of mining families.

An engineer's delight

Whether or not you are an engine lover, it's hard to be unimpressed by the massive 75-cm (30-inch) beam engine which extends up three floors of the mine building – watch

its huge piston rods and wheel in motion. A few minutes' walk away is an even larger 225-cm (90-inch) engine used to pump water from the mine's murky depths (not working).

Did you know?

Boys from the age of 9 went down the mines with their fathers, while their mothers and sisters worked on sorting the rocks. Ask the guides to tell you more about these tight-knit communities.

What can you do?

- Go to the Industrial Heritage Discovery Centre, where you can watch a film – in a proper film theatre – which tells you about the geology of the area, and has footage from the 1900s.
- Buy metal ingots from the shop.

By the way...

There's a lift which takes disabled visitors up and down the engine house.

Cotehele House & Quay

Historic house   Garden   Mill   Quay   Craft gallery   Walks

Going to Cotehele is like travelling back in time. This magical house is hidden away in the Tamar valley, reached down a network of narrow lanes. There are no electric lights, so a tour through the dimly lit rooms can be an exciting experience.

There are some lovely walks through the woods, in the gardens and down to the quay. The unique atmosphere of Cotehele and the friendly stewards and staff make it worth putting aside a whole day for your visit.

St Dominick, nr Saltash,
Cornwall PL12 6TA
Tel (01579) 351346

On W bank of Tamar,
1ml W of Calstock by
steep footpath, 8ml SW
of Tavistock.
Calstock station
$1^1/_2$ ml (uphill).
Bus: First Western
National 79
Callington–Tavistock.

What can you see?
- A whale's jawbones in the Tudor great hall.
- Lots of medieval armour.
- A working water-mill, a medieval dovecote, and a Victorian summer-house.
- Woodpeckers and other wildlife in the woods.

What can you do?
- The walk to the quay, down fairly steep wooded slopes, is quite charming. The trees are enormous and mossy so you feel you are enclosed in a magic world.
- The quay also has a lost-in-time feel: the restored sailing barge *Shamrock* is moored on the quietly lapping, tidal waters of the Tamar. It's hard to imagine this was once a hubbub of trading activity.
- Take a trip on the little boat to Calstock quay (one hour round trip, subject to tides, May to September).

By the way...
Wear sensible shoes.

A bedpost in the King Charles Room

Dunster Castle

Castle   Parkland   Walks

Dunster, nr Minehead,
Somerset TA24 6SL
Tel (01643) 821314

In Dunster, 3ml SE of
Minehead. Dunster
station 1ml.

Family ticket

This fantasy castle with its fairy-tale turrets and towers is largely a 19th-century recreation. Enjoy walks in the parkland around it. Children will have fun spooking themselves out in the dungeons.

Tall tale

In the 1870s workmen found a 2.3-metre (7-foot) skeleton in what was known as an 'oubliette' – a tiny cell in which a prisoner was locked away and forgotten about. No one knows whom the skeleton belonged to or how long it had been there.

What can you see?

- It's worth a crick in the neck to have a really good look at the intricate plasterwork ceiling of the dining room, which dates from 1681.

- Badgers, field mice and even adders sunning themselves on the rocks by the river.

What can you do?

- Children can poke their heads into the secret compartment (probably a priest's hole) off King Charles's Bedroom. It may have connected with a passage to the village – local elderly people remember playing in such a passage when they were young.
- Take a picnic and sit under the stunning 300-year-old oak tree after wearing everyone out with activity sheet and quizzes.

Special events

Dunster Castle hosts some great events. Check for details.

By the way...

The castle is a steep 10-minute climb from the car park. There's transport for those who need it.

Dyrham Park

Historic house Garden Deer park

There's a welcoming atmosphere at Dyrham Park on a Sunday afternoon, with lots of relaxed families picnicking on the grass in front of the house. Search for the furry maple, and other oddly named trees, and head down to the fascinating 19th-century 'below stairs' rooms.

Double Dutch

Look out for all things Dutch in the house, such as blue-and-white Delft china and lots of tulips. The reason? The house was built *c.* 1700 for William Blathwayt, Secretary at War to Dutchman, King William III.

What can you see?

- A clever trick painting by the Dutch artist Samuel van Hoogstraeten. It'll really confuse everyone!
- The fascinating Victorian 'below stairs' rooms. You'll get a good idea of how hard servants worked when you see the huge kitchen ranges and other equipment.
- Peacocks and fallow deer in the park and some wonderful sounding trees – the 'strangle tree', the 'lanky lime' and the 'furry maple'.

What can you do?

- Imagine you're Sarah Saunders, the housekeeper here in 1710. She wrote down every single item in the house for an inventory. What a task!
- Go for a park walk and hoard your precious findings in a paper bag.

Special events

Dyrham occasionally runs family events. Check for details.

By the way...

Treat your kids to a children's book illustrated by Ben Blathwayt, a descendant of the first owner – it's on sale in the shop.

Nr Chippenham, Gloucestershire SN14 8ER
Tel (01179) 372501

8ml N of Bath; 12ml E of Bristol off A46.
Bus: Cotswold Link X55 and Dyrham Shuttle X56 (from Bath).

Family ticket

Finch Foundry

Mill   Museum   River walks

Sticklepath, Okehampton,
Devon EX20 2NW
Tel (01837) 840046

4ml E of Okehampton
off A30. Okehampton
station 4¹/₂ ml.
Bus: Western
National X 9/10.

The enterprising Finch brothers set up their foundry in 1814 to make mining and agricultural tools. Today it's an exciting place for a day out – how often do you get the chance to experience a 19th-century water-powered forge in action?

Nose to the grindstone

Four hundred tools a day were sharpened on the grinding stone here. You can see how workers had to lie flat across the stone wheel to get their tools to it. In winter it was so cold dogs were trained to sit on the men's legs to keep them warm!

What can you see?

- Three water wheels driving the huge tilt hammer and grinding stone.
- An exhibition about the tools made here; see a Devon potato chopper, swan neck hoe and prong digger – sounds nasty!
- Have a look inside Tom Pearce's thatched summer-house, named after the character in the Ballad of Widdicombe Fair.

What can you do?

- Live demonstrations every hour by volunteer demonstrators, and by professional blacksmiths two days a week, will hold the attention of curious children.
- Pick up the 'four villages trail' leaflet for a lovely circular walk which can start at the foundry.
- Children can have fun splashing about in the stream at nearby Billy Green.

Special events

There's an Easter egg hunt every year. Check for future details.

Glendurgan Garden

Garden Maze

Mawnan Smith,
nr Falmouth, Cornwall
TR11 5JZ
Tel (01326) 250906

4ml SW of Falmouth,
$^1/_2$ ml SW of Mawnan
Smith on road to
Helford Passage.
Penmere station 4ml.

Family ticket

Restless children will find plenty to help them let off steam at Glendurgan. There's a laurel maze and the fantastic 'Giant's Stride' maypole. You can also reach the picturesque sandy beach of Durgan through these delightful sub-tropical gardens.

Beaching it

There's a 20-minute walk to reach the tiny hamlet of Durgan and beach. It has good swimming and rock pools, and you can go on a pleasure boat trip, weather permitting.

What can you see?

- Weird sub-tropical plants like giant rhubarb. The enormous tulip tree was called canoe wood by Native Americans, as they could carve a canoe out of a single trunk.
- If you are lucky, one of the rough-legged buzzards.

What can you do?

- Try to lose – or find – your friends in the intricate laurel maze. It is 1 metre (3 feet) high, so taller children will have a bit of an advantage.
- Swing your way on one of the six ropes around the Giant's Stride – it's great for your arm muscles!
- From Durgan hamlet walk to Helford Passage where you can hire all kinds of boats for a trip up the Helford River.

Killerton

Historic house   Costume museum   Discovery centre   Garden   Park

Broadclyst, Exeter,
Devon EX5 3LE
Tel (01392) 881345

On W side of
Exeter–Cullompton road
(B3181). Exeter Central &
St David's stations 7ml.
Bus: Stagecoach Devon
54/A.

Family ticket

If you're in Devon with children, don't miss a visit to Killerton. There's masses to do here from playing with Victorian toys to exploring the park and woods, and there are plenty of excellent quizzes and guides to keep everyone entertained. If you believe the stories, Killerton has its very own dragon....

A bit of history

The present house at Killerton was built in the 18th century for the Acland family who have lived in Devon for 800 years.

What can you see?

● The Victorian laundry, with mangles and irons.
● The costume collection, which has more than 9,000 intriguing outfits.
● The Bear House, once home to the family pet, a not-so-cuddly Canadian black bear!

What can you do?

● The discovery centre is nearly always open in the school holidays (but best to check). This is the heart of the action, where exciting historical and environmental activities are free and change every day. There's an interactive CD-ROM to play with too.
● 'Mrs Craggs' the housekeeper and 'Isabella' the laundry maid invite you for a tour of their part of the house on Wednesdays and Thursdays respectively.
● Follow in the footsteps of globe-trotting 'plant hunters' by searching out the exotic plants and trees brought to Killerton in the 19th century.

Special events

Killerton hosts lots of family events throughout the year from the 'Dragon's Walk' to 'Animal Storytelling'.

Lacock Abbey, Museum & Village

Historic house   Garden   Museum   Village

'Say Cheese'! This phrase probably wouldn't be so familiar if William Henry Fox Talbot hadn't taken the first negative photo here in 1835. Find out more about the history of photography in the museum and visit Talbot's home, Lacock Abbey.

Lacock,
nr Chippenham,
Wiltshire SN15 2LG
Tel (01249) 730459
(museum)
730227 (abbey)

3ml S of Chippenham,
just E of A350.
Chippenham station
3$\frac{1}{2}$ ml.
Bus: First
Badgerline 234/7.

Family ticket

A true story

In the 16th century Olive Sharington jumped off the tower at Lacock Abbey because her father wouldn't let her marry the man she loved. Her skirt acted like a parachute and she floated safely down, landing on top of her loved one and knocking him out! PS Her father relented....

What can you see?

- In the museum, see the tiny print of the Abbey's oriel window, a copy of the first negative photograph.
- Search the Abbey for a skeleton and a goat with a sugar lump on his nose.
- Picturesque medieval half-timbered houses in the village. Not surprisingly, Lacock has starred in TV and film productions such as *Emma* and *Moll Flanders.*

What can you do?

- Explore the Abbey with help from the children's quiz.

- Enjoy a picnic in the field opposite the museum where there's a small play area.

Special events

Young visitors have recently enjoyed adventures with Trusty, woodland trails, an Easter egg hunt, colouring and activities weekends, and a *Water Babies* production.

Lanhydrock

Historic house   Adventure playground   Park   Walks

Bodmin, Cornwall
PL30 5AD
Tel (01208) 73320

2$\frac{1}{2}$ ml SE of Bodmin,
follow signs from A30,
A38 or B3268.
Bus: First Western
National 55 from Bodmin
Parkway (3ml).

The atmosphere of Lanhydrock House is captivating. With the table set for dinner and nightclothes laid out in the Night Nursery, you half expect the Robartes family and their guests to walk in at any moment.

Its 49 rooms are stuffed full of fascinating objects. They range from the dainty boudoir and manly smoking room to well-equipped kitchens and larders, which are what children usually like best. The wooden adventure playground is a real winner and the park offers some beautiful walks.

What can you see?
- Some amazing hunting trophies: a massive moose head, two huge tiger-skin rugs and a mighty pike!
- A 1920s portable tea-making kit for chilly picnics, complete with mini copper teapot and warmer.
- Rabbit and grouse hanging in the larder – are they real?
- A Day Nursery packed with original Victorian toys.

What can you do?
- There is a great adventure playground, which is just the place to let off steam when the children have had enough of the house (don't miss it, it's tucked out of the way at the end of the

car park). There is a wobbly bridge, monkey bars, stepping stones and scramble net ... all surrounded by charming wooden animal sculptures.

- Little tots will enjoy rolling down the many grassy slopes in the gardens at the front of the house.
- The landscaped grounds make a lovely setting for walks (leaflets are available).
- Try the yummy ice-creams made from real Cornish cream sold near the stables and in the car park.

By the way...

There's a 600-metre ($1/_3$-mile) walk from the car park to the house, or you can do the distance in a chauffeur-driven classic car – for a fee! There is a car park for disabled visitors closer by.

Special events

There are always lots of events at Lanhydrock, from all kinds of family environmental days to bat walks, bug hunts and open-air theatre.

Lydford Gorge

River   Waterfall   Walks

The Stables, Lydford Gorge, Lydford, nr Okehampton, Devon EX20 4BH
Tel (01822) 820441

At W end of Lydford village, halfway between Okehampton and Tavistock. 1ml W of A386.
Bus: First Western National 86, and 187 (Sunday, summer only).

Reduced entry charge for those arriving by bus or bike.

Lydford Gorge is a 1$\frac{1}{2}$-mile ravine scooped out of the local rock and peaty soil by the River Lyd which rushes through whirlpools, down a deafening waterfall and along an ancient oak-wooded valley.

What can you see?

- The hundreds of different creatures who have made their home here. Look for lizards, badgers, butterflies – even deer.
- Mini-beasts hidden in piles of wood. NT wardens don't tidy up fallen trees – they are homes for insects which provide food for birds.
- Check the leaf display at the entrance to identify the different trees at Lydford.

What can you do?

- Spectacular short circular walks will guide you through different sections of the gorge. Leaflets are available at the shop.
- 'Walk the plank' over the Devil's Cauldron, the wildest whirlpool on the river.
- Watch for birds at the hide located on the Railway Walk (perfect for pushchairs).

What can you hear?

- The thunderous White Lady waterfall which cascades 30 metres (100 feet).
- The song of chaffinches and warblers in the calmer stretches of the river.

Special events

Recent visitors have enjoyed the Fungus Foray and storytelling.

By the way...

Please take care – the sides of the ravine can be steep and slippery and are not suitable for pushchairs.

Overbecks

Historic house   Museum   Garden

Your family will love Overbecks, an elegant Edwardian house overlooking the sea; it is full of extraordinary objects collected by Otto Overbeck, a scientist and inventor. Staff have made a real effort to interest visiting children and there is plenty for them to do, including searching for Fred the friendly ghost.

Shocking story

Overbeck invented a machine he called 'the popular rejuvenator' which was meant to make people feel younger by giving them an electric shock. Check it out in the Overbecks Room. In the 1920s this sort of eccentric invention was very popular.

What can you see?

- Sharks' teeth, a crocodile skull, birds' eggs and even hyena droppings can be found in Overbeck's weird and wonderful natural history collection.
- Dolls, dolls' houses and toy soldiers.

What can you do?

- Earn a ghost hunter's certificate by finding Fred the ghost. There's a chocolate version of him in the shop.
- Follow clues to the secret children's room crammed with old games and toys.

- Ask to hear the polyphon – a gigantic old-fashioned record player.
- Add your own picture to the children's gallery in the secret room.

By the way...

There's a braille ghost hunt too, for partially-sighted visitors.

Sharpitor, Salcombe,
Devon TQ8 8LW
Tel (01548) 842893

1$\frac{1}{2}$ ml SW Salcombe.
Salcombe station 1$\frac{1}{2}$ ml.
Bus: First Western National
92, and 164 (Sunday only),
Tally Ho! 606.

Family ticket

Leonard Rosoman's portrait of Otto Overbeck with his rejuvenator: an experiment not to be tried at home!

South West

St Michael's Mount

Castle   Church   Coast

Marazion, nr Penzance,
Cornwall TR17 OEF
Tel (01736) 710507

1/2 ml S of A394 at
Marazion, from where
there is access on foot
over the causeway at low
tide, or by ferry at high
tide in the summer. Tide
and ferry info: (01736)
710265. Penzance
station 3ml. Bus: First
Western National 2
Penzance–Falmouth.

Magical tales of giants and an archangel surround this medieval castle on an island off Cornwall's south coast. The beautiful walk to the top is an event in itself. Walk across at low tide, or catch the ferry when it's high.

Jack the Giant Killer

Legend has it that the mount was built by Giant Cormoran, who had a nasty habit of stealing people's sheep for his tea. Jack, a local boy, tried to catch him by digging a deep hole on the path to the castle. He woke the giant with his horn and the sleepy Cormoran fell straight in!

What can you see?

- A crossbow that uses pebbles for shot.

- The door to the dungeon – in the church where they found the skeleton of a man more than 2.3 metres (7-feet) tall. Could it be Cormoran?

What can you do?

- On the climb up to the castle, put your foot on the heart-shaped stone and your right hand on your heart. Can you feel Cormoran's heart beating up through your foot?
- Make a wish on the wishing stone by the church steps – it's the highest point of the island.
- Have a go at the quiz book (for older children).
- Attend the short non-denominational service in the church on Sunday mornings at 11am.

By the way...

The ground is steep and rough in places, and unsuitable for pushchairs. Wear sensible shoes.

Stourhead

Historic house Garden Lake Park

Stourhead's majestic landscaped garden has plenty to offer families – there's lots of open space to run around in and children will have fun searching for the mini-temples and spooky grotto, deliberately built as a ruin to thrill 18th-century visitors. The house is worth a visit too.

Stourton, Warminster,
Wiltshire BA12 6QD
Tel (01747) 841152

Off B3092, 3ml NW of
Mere; 8ml S of Frome.
Gillingham station 6$\frac{1}{2}$ ml;
Bruton station 7ml.
Bus: Wilts & Dorset 26,
Brue Travel 125,
Southern National 59.

Family ticket

Ancient history

Stourhead House and buildings and statues in the gardens were inspired by ancient Greece and Rome – the latest fashion in the 18th century.

What can you see?

- Little follies and buildings around the lake. See if the children can find Hercules in the Pantheon and the River God in the grotto.
- Wild animals such as roe deer and buzzards in the garden, depending on the time of year.
- The 'pole screens' in the Music Room in Stourhead House. These stopped ladies' make-up from melting in the fire's heat.
- Check out the view from Alfred's Tower (3$\frac{1}{2}$ miles from the house).

What can you do?

- Let the children's quiz sheet take you round the house.

- Search for the chamber pot in a secret compartment in the Little Dining Room.
- Walk around the lake and breathe in the calm.

Special events

Stourhead hosts lots of events such as attic and cellar tours and the famous *fête-champêtre* in July when you're the odd one out if you don't dress up.

Studland Beach

Beach Walks Nature reserve

Studland, Swanage,
Dorset BH19 3AX
Tel (01929) 450259

Branksome or Parkstone
stations 3½ml to Shell
Bay or 6ml to Studland
via vehicle ferry.
Bus: Wilts & Dorset
150/152, Yellow Buses
12 then ferry.

Take the children for a fabulous day out on this safe and friendly sandy beach which stretches three miles from South Haven Point to Old Harry Rocks. Middle beach, reached from Knoll or Middle car parks, is particularly good for families.

What can you see?
- Miles of golden sands and blue sea. The shallow water is perfect for bathing.
- All sorts of wildlife such as sea birds swooping over the water, deer in the dunes and even lizards and snakes.

What can you do?
- Bring a picnic and buckets and spades and spend the whole day on the sands.
- If you're feeling more lively, take a self-guided nature walk or meander your way through the nature reserve behind the beach.

Special events
In the summer holidays wardens lead children's beach discovery walks or storytelling sessions.

By the way...
The visitor centre at Knoll car park has information, and other services such as lavatories and a café. There's a designated naturist beach at Studland to head for or avoid!

Trelissick Garden

Garden   Beach   River

These beautiful gardens are a treat. With glorious views down to Falmouth and the open sea, Trelissick makes a great place for a day's outing with a picnic. It is home to all kinds of exotic plants such as skunk cabbage and Australian tree ferns – and is particularly famous for its spring flowers and huge collection of hydrangeas.

What can you see?
- The charming brook which babbles through the watercress beds in Namphillow Wood.
- The tiny escape ladders built for hedgehogs who have fallen into the cattle grids!
- Cormorants, kingfishers and shelduck along the river. (Why do cormorants stand with their wings open?)
- The Celtic Cross summer-house, from where a priest would preach out over the waters to the fishermen.
- Lichen on the fallen logs – did you know lichen won't grow if the air is polluted?

What can you do?
- Work out the time using the sundial in the parsley garden (and practise your Roman numerals).
- Picnic on the lawns across the bridge from the Dell – it's a stunning spot.
- Take the woodland walk along the river edge.

Special events
There are activities for children throughout the year, from Easter egg hunts and theatrical events during the summer to Christmas celebrations.

Feock, nr Truro, Cornwall TR3 6QL
Tel (01872) 862090

4ml S of Truro on both sides of B3289 above King Harry Ferry. Truro station 5 ml. Bus: T7 from Truro.

South West

Trerice

Historic house   Museum   Orchard

Nr Newquay, Cornwall
TR8 4PG
Tel (01637) 875404

3ml SE of Newquay
via A392 and A3058.
Quintrell Downs
station 1$^1/_2$ ml.

Family ticket

Trerice has a great reputation for making families feel welcome. There's a toddlers' corner in the tearoom and children win stickers for doing the quizzes. There's a teapot which looks like a duck, and dragons lurking. The gardens and orchard are very pretty, with all kinds of varieties of old Cornish apple trees.

What can you see?

- Two lions guarding the house – or are they?
- 'Dummy boards' of a boy and girl by the fireplace – used to keep real children company in dimly lit houses.
- The famous Mower Museum may not sound like a major children's attraction, but recently the staff built a 2.4-metre (8-foot) creature called 'Lord Screwloose of Trerice' out of old lawnmower parts! It's worth seeing what their next project is....

What can you do?

- Let the staff lead you 'up the garden path' with their garden trail, or do the house quizzes for both young and older children.
- While parents enjoy a much deserved cuppa, toddlers can scribble and play in their own special corner in the tearoom in the barn.

Special events

There is usually an Easter egg hunt. Check for details of further events.

Ashridge Estate

Countryside Walks Visitor centre

There is wildlife galore in this fabulous area (1,820 hectares/4,500 acres) of woods, chalk downland and common along the ridge of the Chiltern Hills. Take a picnic on a sunny day or crunch through autumn leaves on a woodland walk – it's always delightful.

Ringshall, Berkhamsted, Hertfordshire HP4 1LT
Tel (01442) 851227

Between Northchurch and Ringshall just off B4506.
Tring station 2ml; Berkhamsted station 4ml.
Bus to Monument: Seamarks 27 and 327, Lucketts 30/1. Bus to Beacon: Arriva The Shires 61, Seamarks 327 summer Sundays.

What can you see?

- Wildlife including deer and, if you're lucky, badgers.
- Take your binoculars to spot lesser-spotted woodpeckers and other woodland birds.
- Carpets of spring bluebells among the beech trees.
- Stroll up to the Ivinghoe Beacon on a clear day and see for miles.

What can you do?

- For a small fee, climb the Monument, built in 1832 to commemorate the Duke of Bridgewater, 'Father of inland navigation'.

- Aim for the holidays and join in with fun wildlife activities.

Special events

Recent visitors have made lanterns and forest puppets with an environmental artist. There are family wildlife workshops, Easter egg trails and deer-watching sessions. Contact the visitor centre.

By the way...

The visitor centre is open in the afternoons from April to end October – except on Fridays. Beware – the toilets are shut on Fridays too.

Basildon Park

Historic house   Park   Walks

Lower Basildon, Reading,
Berkshire RG8 9NR
Tel (0118) 984 3040

Between Pangbourne
and Streatley, 7ml NW
of Reading on W side
of A329. Pangbourne
station 2¹/₂ ml.

Family ticket

Basildon Park, a house built in
the 18th-century neoclassical
style, is a good choice for a
Sunday excursion. There's
plenty of space to run around
and everyone will enjoy
glorious walks through the
parkland or on the surrounding
downland and in the woods at
Streatley Hill.

Sticky fingers

There are objects here which
visitors are allowed to touch
and feel. This is unusual for an
NT house – fragile items
usually need protecting.

What can you see?

- Monkeys, elephants, a
  leopard and lots of other
  beasts on a new jungle
  mural covering the walls and
  ceiling of the Small Tearoom.
- An octagonal room with
  highly coloured Indian
  scenes on the walls and a
  ceiling populated with
  eastern birds.
- The stone dogs on the lawn,
  brought back from Italy in
  the 19th century.

What can you do?

- Touch the patterns in the
  Shell Room – a very trendy

Track this man down in the Shell Room.

idea in the 18th century.
- Try one of the walks through
  the park. You'll find a leaflet
  in the ticket office, or follow
  the red posts for a short
  walk, green posts for a
  longer one.
- See if there are any mini-
  beasts in the dead tree in
  Pheasant Park. It's been left
  there to encourage creepy-
  crawlies!

Special events

Basildon Park hosts a few
events for families, particularly
the live crafts show with
demonstrations and
entertainers and children's
theatre events.

Bateman's

Historic house   Garden   Water-mill

Does your family like *The Jungle Book* or *Just So Stories*? This is where their creator, Rudyard Kipling, lived. See drawings of Mowgli and Shere Khan, and Kipling's study just as he left it – with his pipe in the ashtray and his pen awaiting him. From the window of the West Bedroom you can see the hill which was the setting for his book *Puck of Pook's Hill*.

Why Why?

Kipling's elder daughter was called 'Elsie Why?' because she was always asking questions.

What can you see?

- The original illustrations for *The Jungle Book* drawn by Kipling's father.
- The initials that the Kipling family carved into their porch one rainy afternoon.
- The family Rolls Royce, still standing in the garage.

What can you do?

- Try the children's quiz.
- Visit the water-mill which generated electricity for the whole house.

Special events

Every year there's a book day with East Sussex libraries. Check for details.

By the way...

Kipling designed the garden pond himself, making it especially shallow so that children could fall in safely – but please don't put it to the test!

Burwash, Etchingham, East Sussex TN19 7DS
Tel (01435) 882302

1/2 ml S of Burwash (A265). Etchingham station 3ml

Family ticket

Bodiam Castle

Castle   Moat   Parkland

Bodiam, nr
Robertsbridge,
East Sussex TN32 5UA
Tel (01580) 830436

3m S of Hawkhurst,
1m E of B2244.
Robertsbridge
station 5ml.
Bus: Fuggles/Stagecoach
South Coast 349 from
Tunbridge Wells to
Hastings station.

Family ticket

Have a go at trying on medieval armour in this fantastic
14th-century castle, one of the most famous and atmospheric
in Britain. We guarantee children will love it here.

What can you see?
- The original garderobes (medieval lavatories).
- Murder holes in the roof of the gatehouse where people dropped boiling water or quicklime to stop the enemy getting in.
- A Second World War pill box.

What can you do?
- Try on the sort of armour Bodiam soldiers wore. There are even adult-sized outfits – check the education room is open, though.
- Pretend to be look-outs high up on the battlements.
- Feed the ducks on the pond.
- Walk the battlements.

Special events
There's always lots going on at Bodiam, from medieval weekends (where you can

have a go with an authentic bow and arrow) to children's books days and Easter egg trails. There are lovely open-air concerts for the adults, too. Children can even have a medieval birthday party dressed up in costume.

By the way...

Bodiam is often used by school groups in the mornings during term time. To avoid unhappy children going home without trying on the armour, please ring in advance to check it is available.

Box Hill

Countryside   Walks   Information centre

The Old Fort, Box Hill
Road, Box Hill, Tadworth,
Surrey KT20 7LB
Tel (01306) 885502

1ml N of Dorking; 2$\frac{1}{2}$ ml.
S of Leatherhead on A24.
Boxhill and Westhumble
station $\frac{1}{2}$ ml.
Bus: Arriva Surrey & W
Sussex 516.

You can't beat flying a kite on a billowy day on Box Hill with
its fabulous views over the South Downs. If you're up there on
a Saturday afternoon, why not play games on the wide open
spaces of the chalky downland or stretch your legs walking
through beautiful woods?

Why Box Hill?

The box tree, which has a
smell reminiscent of tomcats,
has grown here in abundance
since at least the 16th century.
Box Hill has been a beauty
spot for at least as long. Jane
Austen located her ill-fated
picnic here in her novel *Emma*.
We hope you have a better
time!

What can you see?

- Wildlife including 40 species
  of butterflies, birds such as
  tawny owls and kestrels, roe
  deer, badgers and foxes.
  If you can't see them, you
  might spot some of their
  tracks.
- There's wild strawberry,
  bee orchids, rock rose and
  a thousand other delightful
  flowers.

What can you do?

- Energetic families can go for a walk. Excellent leaflets are available in the information centre on the summit, including a 2-mile nature trail via Juniper Bottom.
- Dare to touch natural exhibits, such as a prickly birds' nest and a badger skull, in an interactive display at the information centre.

Special events

A host of outdoor events take place every year at Box Hill. Ring the number above to find out details.

By the way...

You can buy drinks and snacks at the Servery, but it isn't a fully fledged restaurant with lots of services.

Stepping stones over the River Mole, on North Downs Way.

Claremont Landscape Garden

Gardens   Lake   Amphitheatre

Portsmouth Road, Esher,
Surrey KT10 9JG
Tel (01372) 467806

On S edge of Esher, on E
side of A307. Esher,
Hersham and Claygate
stations all 2ml.
Bus: Arriva Surrey &
W Sussex 415.

Family ticket

Claremont is a tranquil oasis in urban Surrey, and a landscape garden surviving from the 18th century. There's a strong chance that in the woods you will bump into Princess Charlotte, daughter of George IV who lived here in the early 19th century! The staff have recently introduced colourful cut-outs of key historical figures into the grounds.

Gardeners' world

Some of the country's greatest gardeners created Claremont – Sir John Vanbrugh, Charles Bridgeman and 'Capability' Brown, to name but a few.

What can you see?

● Do you know your black swan from your greylag goose? Spot some of the 52 species of waterfowl on the lake using the bird guide – a great family favourite.

What can you do?

● Claremont is particularly handy for young children, as the lake is close to the car park – so you can just drop in to feed the ducks.
● There's also plenty for a whole day's outing, including the children's trail, the walk round the lake (suitable for buggies) and nature trail.
● Climb the mound and spot

creepy-crawlies in the trees which fell in the 1987 storm.

Special events

There's an Easter egg hunt each year, and special children's trails and Trusty walks in the holidays. In July, there's a spectacular *fête-champêtre* when you must all dress up.

By the way...

Dogs are only allowed from November until the end of March.

Claydon House

Historic house   Museum   Park   Lake

Exotic 18th-century carvings of oriental birds and scaly monsters fill this intriguing house. You can also see the room Florence Nightingale stayed in when she visited her sister.

Gruesome tale

Sir Edmund Verney, the first owner of Claydon, was King Charles I's standard-bearer. At the battle of Edgehill in 1642 his hand was chopped off by Cromwell's Roundheads so that they could seize the King's flag. The rest of his body was never found – it had completely vanished. Some say his ghost still haunts the house looking for his hand.

What can you see?

- Letters Florence Nightingale wrote to her sister describing the awful conditions in the Crimean War.
- A massive 19th-century Javanese gamelan in the museum.
- The mythical phoenix on top of the Verney coat of arms and scaly wyverns scattered around the house.

- 18th-century carvings that look good enough to eat – especially the tea party in the Chinese Room.

What can you do?

- In the North Hall, touch and feel some of Claydon's amazing carvings and the collection of household items from candle snuffs to jelly moulds.
- Ask in the Museum Room to hear a cassette of gamelan music.
- Take a tour of the museum with the children's quiz.

Special events

Outdoor theatre and music, and guided tours of the park take place at Claydon. Check for details.

Middle Claydon,
nr Buckingham,
Buckinghamshire
MK18 2EY
Tel (01296) 730349

13m NW of Aylesbury;
$3^1/_2$ ml SW of Winslow.
Bus: 17 from
Aylesbury station.

Family ticket

Dapdune Wharf & River Wey Navigations

Old barge   Exhibition   River

Wharf Road, Guildford,
Surrey GU1 4RR
Tel (01483) 561389

On Wharf Road to rear
of cricket ground off
Woodbridge Road
(A332), Guildford.
Also access from town
centre on foot via
towpath or on river bus.
Access to rest of
Navigations from A3 and
M25.
Addlestone, Byfleet &
New Haw, Guildford,
Farncombe & Godalming
stations all close to
Navigations.

Family ticket

Back in 1653 the Wey was one of the first rivers to be made navigable and today, with its barges and riverways, it's a great place for families. You can clamber aboard *Reliance*, a restored barge, at Dapdune Wharf in Guildford. Or take to the water on the River Wey in all kinds of ways – from punts to narrow boats – or try one of the beautiful circular walks along its towpaths.

What can you see?

- All kinds of wildlife along the River Wey towpath (the stretch between Walsham Gates and Papercourt is best).
- Walk around the inside of the old barge *Reliance* and see what life was like for the bargemen.

What can you do?

- Press buttons, touch screens and shine torches underwater at the exhibition at Dapdune Wharf.
- Have a go at the family trail 'Wally's Wharf Walk' at Dapdune Wharf.
- Take the 20-minute river bus trip on the *Dapdune Bell* (additional charge).
- Go fishing on the River Wey. Permits can be obtained from the Environment Agency or one of the angling clubs. (Staff at the Navigations Office can advise.)

Special events

At Dapdune Wharf there are pirate parties and treasure hunts on summer weekends and in the summer holidays; Easter egg hunts and environmental activity days in the Easter holidays. From November to March take guided walks along the Navigations.

By the way...

The machinery on the Wharf is fragile, so please respect signs asking you not to climb on it.

Devil's Dyke

Countryside Walks

Devil's Dyke is a delightful spot on the South Downs where on a fine day you can take in breathtaking views of up to 20 miles with the help of a pay-to-see telescope. Enjoy a day out in the fresh air with kite-flyers, dogs and walkers and create your own stories for how the area got its name.

The Devil's tale
The dramatic valley cut into the chalk was supposedly dug by the Devil who wanted the incoming sea to drown the many churches in the Weald. He had until sunrise to complete his dastardly task but a candle in the window of a house and a crowing cockerel made him think the night was over, and he abandoned his project.

What can you see?
- Information panels explaining the great views.
- Dare-devil hang-gliders floating through the sky.
- Measure out a square metre (yard) of downland and you could find 50 different plants and sweet-smelling herbs. Spot exotic orchids and gentians too.

What can you do?
- Take a bike ride along the bridlepaths.
- Wander off on self-guided walks aimed at rambling families in the 'Delve into the Downs' leaflet.

Special events
Ugly Bug Safaris and Devil's Dyke Detectives and more. Check for details.

By the way...
Tuck into lunch at the child-friendly pub by the car park.

Devil's Dyke, Estate Office, Saddlescombe Farm, Brighton, West Sussex BN45 7DE
Tel (01273) 857712

Off A23, nr Poynings, N of Brighton.

Gateway to the White Cliffs & South Foreland Lighthouse

Langdon Cliffs, nr Dover,
Kent CT16 1HJ
Tel (01304) 202756

Follow brown signs from
roundabout 1ml NE of
Dover at jct of A2/A258.
Dover Priory station
2¹/₂ ml.
Bus: Stagecoach
East Kent 100.

The White Cliffs of Dover are known the world over. The NT protects this impressive landscape for everyone for ever. Children are especially welcome and there is a new visitor centre from which to start an exploration of the cliff tops. The splendid South Foreland Lighthouse is a 30-minute walk away.

What can you see?

- Exmoor ponies who graze the cliffs and so protect the flower and insect life.
- If you go down to one of the little bays on the shore you can investigate the rock pools if the tide is right. There are also shipwrecks to discover (the Channel is the world's busiest shipping lane).

An early 20th-century wreck below Langdon Cliffs.

What can you do?

- Enjoy a cliff-top walk with breathtaking views out across the Channel.
- Push the buttons and get on the computers at the interactive displays at the visitor centre, which tell you the story of the cliffs.
- Walk along the cliff tops to the South Foreland Lighthouse where you can find out how early radio pioneer Guglielmo Marconi made the world's first ship to shore distress transmission in 1898. (Similar equipment was used by the *Titanic* to try to summon help during her tragic maiden voyage.)

Special events

There are treasure trails and themed guided walks at various times in the year.

Call for further details.

By the way

The visitor centre and a path to the viewpoint are accessible by wheelchair.

Greys Court

Historic houses Tower Garden Maze

Rotherfield Greys,
Henley-on-Thames,
Oxfordshire RG9 4PG
Tel (01491) 628529

3ml W of Henley-on-Thames; take A4130
to Oxford, then B481
from Nettlebed mini-roundabout.
Henley-on-Thames
station 3ml.
Bus: Yellow Bus M1,
Reading Buses 137.

Family ticket

Greys Court is an intriguing property with lots for families to enjoy. There is a beautiful 16th-century house which is interesting but not too large, and, amongst the ruins of a medieval fortified manor, a series of pretty gardens linked by 'doorways' in the walls. There is a maze where children can find their way to the middle with no fear of getting lost, and a medieval tower to climb.

Murder!

In 1613 Robert Carr and his wife Frances, two of James I's favourites, were accused of murdering another courtier, and imprisoned. The King then banished them to Greys Court – not much of a punishment, you might think.

What can you see?

- The Tudor donkey wheel which brought water to the house until 1914.
- A delightful series of 'secret' gardens.

- The ice-house, where ice was stored before the invention of fridges.

What can you do?

- Get lost in the Archbishop's Maze, opened in 1981 by Robert Runcie.
- Take the shortish (about 2 miles) walk around the estate.

Special events

Greys Court hosts a few events each year such as an Easter egg hunt. Check for details.

Hughenden Manor

Historic house Park Woodland Walks

Hughenden Manor was the much loved country home of 19th-century Conservative Prime Minister, Benjamin Disraeli. Enjoy the manor filled with his pictures, books and furniture, and then take the family for a walk in the gardens and surrounding park and woodland. Be warned – it is very hilly in places. There are often extra children's activities going on.

'We Authors, Ma'am'

Disraeli was a great favourite with Queen Victoria, unlike the Liberal Prime Minister, William Gladstone, whom she thought addressed her like a public meeting. Both Disraeli and the Queen had written books – he was a very successful novelist, while she published an account of her travels in Scotland.

What can you see?
- The secret servants' doors in the dining room (if you can find them).
- Disraeli's own books, all 4,000 of them! On the staircase wall is his 'gallery of friendship', with portraits of his many friends, including the Queen and his devoted wife, Mary Anne.
- A marble copy of Mary

continued...

High Wycombe, Buckinghamshire HP14 4LA
Tel (01494) 755573

1½ ml N of High Wycombe on W side of A4128. High Wycombe station 2ml
Bus: Arriva the Shires 323/4 (long steep walk to house).

Family ticket

Anne's foot – the Queen started a craze for this when she had her children's feet sculpted.

- The German forest planted by the Disraelis.

What can you do?

- Use the fun children's guide to explore the house and garden.
- Try out the family story trail – there's a leaflet to guide you on this half-hour walk round the estate.
- Go to the church and see the monument put up by Queen Victoria to her favourite Prime Minister.

- Enjoy a scrumptious lunch or tea in the Stableyard Restaurant.

Special events

There are lots of great events at Hughenden. For details, call the education warden on the above number, or the regional box office on (01494) 755572. There will be a charge for most events.

By the way...

For £5 a day you can hire a super-tough, all-terrain buggy, to negotiate the bumpy ground on the estate walks.

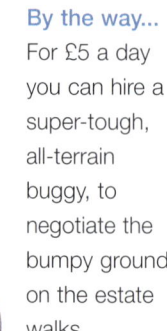

Ightham Mote

Historic house   Walks

Nobody has ever discovered the identity of the skeleton found in a tiny cupboard in the Great Hall. Spooky! Investigate this and other ancient curiosities with a visit to this moated manor house nestling in a secluded valley. It's great for nature lovers too – and in the woods there's a shelter from which to watch the wildlife, and some interesting walks.

A miniature version of the house was provided for Dido the St Bernard, who lived here in the 1890s.

Ivy Hatch, Sevenoaks, Kent TN15 0NT
Tel (01732) 810378
Info line (01732) 811145

6ml E of Sevenoaks, off A25 and 2½ml S of Ightham off A227. Borough Green & Wrotham station 3½ml; Hildenborough station 4ml.
Bus: Tel (03456) 96996.

Family ticket

What can you see?

- The kennel made in 1890 specially for a St Bernard dog who was so big her food had to be served in a washing up bowl.
- The massive sweet chestnut tree which measures over 8 metres (23 feet) around.

What can you do?

- Squint through the squint and have a chat through the parley hole. And what on earth is a putlog?
- Do the woodland quiz – does a centipede really have 100 legs?
- Be a nature detective and work out the age of a tree using the tree ring trick.
- Find all about medieval crafts, from stone-masonry to carpentry.

Special events

Family days are action-packed at Ightham Mote: from prickly encounters with Trusty the Hedgehog, to brass rubbing, face painting, woodcarving demonstrations and games in the courtyard.

By the way...

There is a fun children's corner in the shop.

Needles Old Battery

Fort

West Highdown,
Totland, Isle of Wight
PO39 OJH
Tel (01983) 754772

At Needles Headland,
W of Freshwater Bay
and Alum Bay (B3322).
Ferry from Yarmouth,
E Cowes, Ryde or
Fishborne.
Bus: Island Rover ticket
or 42 from Yarmouth.

Family ticket

A Victorian fort in a stunning position overlooking the Needles. Children with an interest in guns, ships and military matters can get a real feel of what is was like for the soldiers who saw action here in the Second World War.

What can you see?

- The long, and sorry, list of ships that were wrecked on the Needles.
- Cartoons by Geoff Campion which explain what went on at the Old Battery.
- The children's display in the shell store.
- The restored powder store and laboratory.

What can you do?

- Learn to use the Beaufort Scale to work out how strong the wind is.
- Venture down the 60-metre (180-foot) tunnel and emerge at the searchlight position that has a fantastic view out over the Needles.
- Do the children's quiz (one for younger, one for older children), and learn all kinds of things, such as what precautions they took to ensure the room full of gunpowder didn't explode!

Keeps you fit!

It's a 3/4-mile walk up to the Old Battery, which can be hard going for pushchairs.

By the way...

Bembridge Windmill, on the other side of the Isle of Wight, is well worth a visit. It dates from 1700 and is the island's only surviving windmill. Children love climbing up the central staircase to get spectacular views.

One of the illustrations by famous wartime cartoonist Geoff Campion.

Nymans Garden

Garden   Woodland walks

Hedges shaped like well-known chocolate bars and monkey puzzle trees will hold your children's interest on an afternoon's stroll around these splendid Sussex gardens. The Messel family who designed them made sure there is some kind of surprise around every corner.

What can you see?
- Gruesome stone faces peering down at you in the walled garden.
- In the old green shed, photos of the house and people who used to live there.
- The dovecote.
- Exotic shrubs and trees.

What can you do?
- Solve the children's garden quiz – and win a Trusty certificate.
- Visit the topiary in front of the house and outside the Wall Garden. Are they animals or plants?

- Copy the expressions of the stone faces in the little summer-house – and see what your family thinks!
- Follow one of the walks in the woodlands of the surrounding estate.

Special events
Craft fairs and teddy bears' picnics are held in the summer, and there's a craft fair and family fun days at Christmas. Call for details.

Handcross, Haywards Heath, Sussex RH17 6EB
Tel (01444) 400321

On B2114 at Handcross, off London–Brighton M23/A23.
Balcombe station 4$^{1}/_{2}$ ml
Bus: Arriva Surrey & W Sussex 773.

Family ticket

Petworth House

Historic house Park Lake

Petworth,
West Sussex
GU28 OAE
Tel (01798) 342207

In centre of Petworth,
A272/A283. Pulborough
station 5³/₄ ml.

Family ticket

This magnificent late 17th-century house, with its beautiful park landscaped by 'Capability' Brown a hundred years later, makes a great day out for families. The park has more than 1,000 deer – probably the largest herd in Britain. The house is full of treasures, with family portraits and paintings by Turner, who lived at Petworth for several years.

Fancy that!

Elizabeth Percy, who inherited Petworth in 1682, married three times before she was 16. Her third husband, the Duke of Somerset, was so full of his own importance that he cut one of their daughters out of his will because she dared to sit down while he was asleep!

Priority for pets

Look out for the little cemetery for the family pets on the lawn near the North Gallery. There's also a statue of a dog by the lake. It's the 3rd Earl of Egremont's favourite hunting dog which probably drowned.

What can you see?

- One of the National Trust's best collections of paintings.
- Extensive servants' quarters, with kitchens furnished with the latest equipment of the mid-19th century.

- Intricate wooden carvings by Grinling Gibbons in the Carved Room.

What can you do?

- Follow the route servants took from kitchen to dining room, through an underground passage.
- Watch the deer. They seem quite tame, but do try not to disturb them. Fawns standing on their own are very cute but don't be tempted to pick them up – the mother has probably just moved away to get something to eat.

Special events

There's always plenty to do at Petworth. Past events have included storytelling, a craft festival at the end of May and

a kite festival. Check what's on before you visit.

By the way...

There is a great playground by the car park in nearby Petworth.

Above: Fun at the spring plant fair. Left: Ice-creams, Victorian-style, on show in the larder.

Polesden Lacey

Historic house   Garden   Walks

Great Bookham,
nr Dorking, Surrey
RH5 6BD
Tel (01372)
458203/452048

5ml NW of Dorking,
2ml S of Great Bookham,
off A246.
Boxhill & Westhumble
station 2ml.
Bus: Surrey Hills Leisure
433 from Guildford
summer Sundays,
Arriva Surrey & W Sussex
408 Guildford–Croydon.

Family ticket

In a beautiful setting on the North Downs, this Regency villa has some of the best views in Surrey. Have a go at one of the waymarked walks, or play grass games in the picnic area. A real favourite with children is the pet dog cemetery. At the beginning of the 20th century the house belonged to a society hostess, Mrs Greville. Step back into the 1920s, stroll through the house and grounds and imagine you are one of her famous house-guests.

What can you see?

- The mementoes of the guests, kept by Mrs Greville in her special book. You can even find out what they had to eat!

- Walls covered with gilt and a chandelier with nearly 4,000 pieces that takes over a week to clean.
- Some stunning scenery.

Royal connections

The Queen Mother spent part of her honeymoon here.

What can you do?

- Have a bash at croquet on the croquet lawn.
- The woodland trail and house quiz.

Special events

The Polesden Lacey festival, which includes a children's concert and fair with donkey rides, takes place each summer. There are also Countryside Capers for children led by the warden, and croquet coaching afternoons. Check for details.

Sheffield Park Garden

Garden Lakes Walks

Sheffield Park, East
Sussex TN22 3QX
Tel (01825) 790231

Midway between
East Grinstead and
Lewes, 5ml NW of
Uckfield E of A275.
Sheffield Park station
(Bluebell Railway) 1/2 ml;
Uckfield station 6ml;
Haywards Heath 7ml.

Family ticket

Look out for foxes, kingfishers and rabbits in these glorious 50-hectare (120-acre) gardens, with their four lakes linked by cascades and waterfalls.

Spooky waters...

Between the third and fourth lakes there used to be stepping stones creating the 'Woman's Way'. According to legend, a headless woman appears here, but she vanishes into thin air if you approach her.

What can you see?

- Daffodils and bluebells in spring; rhododendrons and azaleas, water lilies and irises in summer; fantastic golden and red colours in the autumn; frosty walks and mists on the lakes in winter.
- Swans, herons, hares, ducks, frogs, dormice and more....
- The massive American trees which survived the 1987 storm on the Big Tree Walk.

What can you do?

- Mug up your tree types with the tree trail.

Special events

Have a go at weaving, spinning and even working the cleaving machine used to make metal tools at a Victorian weekend. Go on a bat walk or a teddy bears' picnic (call the property for details).

By the way...

Be warned that dogs are only allowed in the car park, and on leads. Half a mile up the road is the Bluebell Steam Railway – not NT, but a joint ticketing system has been arranged.

Stowe Landscape Gardens

Garden Park Lakes

Children may tumble about happily in what is really a rather ornate park. No swings and roundabouts – but lots of other attractions in the shape of monuments and temples inspired by ancient Greece and Rome.

What's in a name?

The gardens were laid out in the 18th century by three generations of one family. As the generations married other rich families, so they kept adding to their name – one of the owners was able to call himself Richard Plantagenet Temple-Nugent-Brydges-Chandos-Grenville!

What can you see?

- As you walk around, look out for sudden views of temples and monuments. Stowe was especially designed to keep visitors on their toes.
- The Congreve Monument –

a pyramid with a little monkey perched on top.
- The Grotto where rather damp family parties were held in the 18th century.

What can you do?

- Search for Queen Elizabeth I and William Shakespeare in the Temple of British Worthies in the Elysian Fields. Who else can you find?
- After enjoying a walk around the gardens, pick a picnic spot under one of Stowe's beautiful trees.

Special events

Stowe holds some events, like a spring kite festival and summer model sailing boat regatta, which are great family entertainments.

By the way...

Unfortunately manual wheelchairs cannot be accommodated.

Buckingham,
Buckinghamshire
MK18 5EH
Tel (01280) 822850

3ml NW of Buckingham via Stowe Avenue, off A422.
Bus: From Milton Keynes and Aylesbury to Buckingham town centre, then taxi to Stowe.

Family ticket

South and South East

Witley and Milford Commons

Heaths Woodland Visitor centre

Witley Centre,
Witley, Godalming,
Surrey GU8 5QA
Tel (01428) 683207

7ml SW of Guildford
between A3 and A286
roads. 1ml SW of Milford.
Milford station 2ml.
Bus: Stagecoach Hants &
Surrey/Coastline 60.

Free entry

Wesley the woodpecker and Franky the fox accompany you on the nature trail around this lovely area of heathland and woodland – one of the remaining fragments of the heath that used to cover much of southern England.

It's a great place just to come and enjoy the space and bring a picnic. There are also fun children's activities at the Witley Centre – where you can sit and have tea while you watch birds at the bird table.

What can you see?

- Nightingales and Dartford warblers on Milford Common. Finches, tit, woodpeckers and nuthatches on Witley Common.
- Look closely on the paths and you may find spectacular wood-ant nests, and plenty of fungi in the autumn.
- Expanses of purple heather in late summer.

What can you do?

- Pick up a quiz sheet from the Witley Centre and go on one of the two nature trails.

- See what's on the touch table at the Centre and have a go at the nature puzzles, quizzes and colouring sheets.

Special events

Easter egg trails, outdoor fun days and art and craft days are typical of holiday events at Witley.

Morden Hall Park & Snuff Mill

Waterways Meadows Environmental centre

A green oasis in the heart of London suburbia, this park is a charming spot with meandering streams and weirs, hay meadows and formal gardens. The staff at the Snuff Mill Environmental Centre run all kinds of activities for children. There's also a huge aquatic centre in the garden centre (not NT).

Morden Hall Road,
Morden,
London SM4 5JD
Tel 020 8648 1845

Off A24 and A297 S of Wimbledon. Morden underground station $1/_3$ ml.

Free entry

What can you see?

- Watch out for coots, moorhens and herons on the waterways.
- Fish of all kinds in the 300 aquaria in the garden centre.

What can you do?

- Visit Dene City Farm (free entry) which is run by a charity inside the park. A variety of farm animals can be seen, and there's also pony-riding.

Snuff Mill Environmental Centre

Children who enjoy watching butterflies and river dipping will love the different activities here:

- The Nature Club, run by the NT and the London Wildlife Trust, is held on Saturday mornings, for 6- to 13-year-olds. Booking is essential.
- Explorer Days for 5- to 9-year-olds are held at most half-terms and in school holidays.
- Birthday parties with a natural theme are also available.

Osterley Park

Historic house Lake Park

Jersey Road, Isleworth,
Middlesex TW7 4RB
Tel 020 8568 7714

Osterley underground
station 1/2 ml.

Family ticket

Osterley is a beautiful house in a lovely park within easy reach of central London. Originally built in Tudor times, it was transformed in the 18th century by the architect Robert Adam for the Child family to entertain their rich City friends. Now, it's a haven of peace in the suburbs. Keep an eye out for rabbits and squirrels, and even parakeets, when you play in the park.

Heartbreak house

In 1782 the 18-year-old daughter of the house, Sarah Anne, ran away to Gretna Green to marry the Earl of Westmorland. Soon afterwards her father is said to have died of a broken heart.

What can you see?

- The huge 400-year-old oaks in the park. Some may have been planted by the first owner of Osterley, Sir Thomas Gresham.
- A fantastically flouncy bed in the State Bedroom, also designed by Robert Adam.
- The 16th-century stables which are still in use and open on Sunday afternoons in summer.

What can you do?

- For a small extra cost, the family can join in activity days in the holidays – mini-safaris of the bug-infested meadows, recycling fun and treasure hunts have all been on offer recently.
- Puzzle over the children's quizzes about the house or park.
- Find out what life was like 'below stairs' by exploring the servants' quarters. Check beforehand as they are not always open.
- Search for the marigold – both as a decorative emblem and the real flowers – scattered around the house. This was the Child family symbol.

The state bed, which an 18th-century visitor thought looked like a very theatrical lady's hat.

- Look for the dirty patch on the wall in the Etruscan Room. This gives an idea of the work the National Trust has to do, to keep houses like Osterley looking good.

Special events

There are family fun days throughout the summer and other major events such as the 1930s Christmas party and decorating the Victorian tree. They do get booked up, so contact the education office on 020 8568 4178 to avoid disappointment.

By the way...

There is a discount on the adult entry price to the house for families arriving on public transport. Don't forget to keep your travelcard, though.

Sutton House

Historic house

2&4 Homerton High Street, Hackney, London E9 6JQ
Tel 020 8986 2264

At the corner of Isabella Road and Homerton High Street. Hackney Central station ¹/₄ ml; Hackney Downs station ¹/₂ ml. Bus: Frequent from central London.

Family ticket

Sutton House, a peaceful Tudor brick building in the heart of busy East London, is an unusual NT property but well worth a visit. Discover how the house has developed over the centuries.

A bit of history

The house was built in 1535 by Sir Ralph Sadleir, an up-and-coming Tudor courtier, when Hackney was a pretty village outside London. The house has since been a rich merchant's home, schools for both boys and girls, and, after the rector of St John-at-Hackney bought it in 1890, a recreation centre for poor working men.

What can you see?
● Fine Tudor oak panelling

and carved fireplaces which miraculously survive intact after years of neglect.
● You can open doors and panels to reveal parts of the original Tudor house including two 'garderobe' lavatories.

What can you do?
● Explore the old cellars.
● Find out about life for William Evans, a 13-year-old who lived nearby. He tells his own story in 'Victorian Life in Hackney', an interactive computer programme.

Special events
Join in with a whole host of activities such as historical cooking and drama in the holidays or at the Saturday Kids' Club. Check for details.

By the way...
Sutton House is not open every day – do check before you visit.

Children from nearby schools have a go at Tudor-style embroidery.

Anglesey Abbey

Historic house   Garden   Mill   Play area

Lode, Cambridge
CB5 9EJ
Tel (01223) 811200

6ml NE of Cambridge
on B1102, near the
village of Lode.
Signposted from A14.
Bus: 111/122 from
Cambridge.

Family ticket

Anglesey Abbey is not an abbey but an early 17th-century house built on the site of a priory. Children of all ages enjoy rolling about on the majestic lawns and running down the grassy ditches. These used to be filled with water and were the source of the monks' Friday supper! The water-mill is in full working order, and flour may be bought.

What can you see?
- The house is a jackdaw's heaven. It's jam-packed with tapestries, paintings, and lots of treasures collected by the 1st Lord Fairhaven.
- There are 37 clocks in the house. See if you can spot all of them, and track down other curiosities using the children's guide.

What can you do?
- Turn up on one of the milling days to see the mill in action (call for details).
- There's a small wooden play area in the picnic area for little ones.
- The avenues of trees are excellent hide-and-seek territory (and good for conkers).
- Follow the garden trails.

Special events
There are different Trusty the Hedgehog walks for all seasons. Call for details.

Belton House

Historic house Adventure playground Garden

Grantham, Lincolnshire
NG32 2LS
Tel (01476) 566116

3ml NE of Grantham on
A607 Grantham–Lincoln
road. Grantham station
3ml. Bus: 609
Grantham–Sleaford.

Family ticket

The fantastic woodland adventure playground makes a day out at Belton House a winner for families. As well as the mega-slides and tree houses you would expect from a grand-style playground, there is a special corral for under-6s, and miniature train rides in the summer. There are all kinds of other activities to fascinate children. The 17th-century house is one of the finest country houses in England.

As seen on TV...

Fans of the children's television serial *Moondial* by author Helen Cresswell will particularly enjoy Belton as it was in the house and grounds that the series was filmed – track down the real moondial. The house also appeared in the BBC's serial *Pride and Prejudice* as Lady Catherine de Bourgh's home. It also had a starring role in the 1997 serial, *Tom Jones*.

What can you see?

- The power of the human touch: in the activity room in the house there are fabrics which are half protected and half you can touch, and the difference is...
- The deer which roam in the 400-hectare (1,000-acre) park.
- All the different animals used in the decorations and paintings in the house.

What can you do?

- Swing, climb and slide your way around the mega wilderness adventure playground, while the less energetic can watch from the picnic tables.
- Have fun in the upstairs activity room trying on genuine Victorian clothes – parents can have a go too!
- There's also an outdoor activity room in the stableyard where you can see the nature table and join in various wildlife activities, but ring in advance to see if it is open.

Special events

On Sundays Belton occasionally holds family days with a wide range of extra attractions (no extra admission charge), and painting days for all ages. Ring for details.

Blickling Hall

Historic house   Garden   Lake   Park

Blickling, Norwich,
Norfolk NR11 6NF
Tel (01263) 738030

On N side of B1354,
1½ ml NW of Aylsham
Station. Bus: 53/8, X58
First Eastern Counties
Norwich–Sheringham.

Family ticket

Take your chances to see
Anne Boleyn's ghost at this
beautiful 17th-century mansion,
topped by striking brick
chimneys. The house has
stunning gardens and an 18th-
century landscape park – keep
your eyes open for the
woodpeckers and owls.

Spooky story

Henry VIII's second queen,
Anne Boleyn, lived in an earlier
house at Blickling when she
was young. Her headless
ghost has been seen riding up
to the house in a coach pulled
by headless horses. (Did you
know she had six fingers on
one hand?)

What can you see?

- Anne Boleyn's life-size
  statue on the stairs.
- A long gallery with a plaster
  ceiling showing some very
  curious beasts.
- Secret garden with sundial.
- A pyramid – not Egyptian,
  but the mausoleum of one
  of Blickling's owners.

What can you do?

- The low-hanging trees offer
  plenty of hide-
  and-seek
  opportunities.
- Have a go
  at the garden
  trail.

Special events

There are
lots of special
events – from
Easter egg trails
to family
activity days.
Call for details.

*Ahoy there!
Getting dressed up
at a Blickling
family fun day.*

Dunwich Heath & Minsmere Beach

Beach   Heath   Visitor centre

Dunwich Heath is a remote and beautiful stretch of windy Suffolk coastline with some magnificent views over the sea. There are great beach and heath walks and a chance to spot the wealth of wildlife in the area.

Coastguard Cottages, nr Dunwich, Saxmundham, Suffolk 1P17 3DJ Tel (01728) 648505

1ml S of Dunwich on coast between Aldeburgh and Southwold. Access signposted on A12 at Yoxford and Blythburgh.

What can you see?
- Expanses of heather and gorse, and a beach with a great variety of pebbles.
- The plans showing where Dunwich town used to be – the old town, which was a thriving port in medieval times, has now fallen into the sea!
- The look-out in the information room has some stunning views.

What can you do?
- Listen for nightingales, bittern and stonechats, sand martins, kestrels and linnets.
- Splash in the sea and wander along the sand and shingle of Minsmere Beach.
- Find out about the heath and beach in the look-out in the old coastguard cottages.
- Enjoy a picnic overlooking the sea.

Special events
There are 'holiday club' days in the school holidays when children aged 6 to 12 can take part in all kinds of environmental activities. There are also very popular nature trails, 'Have a Go' family sessions in August which include beach art and gorse shakes.

By the way...
If you fall in love with the area, why not think about hiring one of the Trust's holiday flats?

Felbrigg Hall

Historic house   Park   Walks

Felbrigg, Norwich, Norfolk
NR11 8PR
Tel (01263) 837444

Nr Felbrigg village, 2ml
SW of Cromer off B1436.
Cromer station 2¹/₄ ml.
Bus: From Cromer or
Sheringham summer only.

Family ticket

Find the bath which got you clean without the servants getting the slightest glimpse of your private parts. Spot the false door in the dining room and look up inside a dovecote full of white doves. Felbrigg is a fine 17th-century house surrounded by a park with some stunning trees and plenty of space to run around in.

What can you see?

- Teeny weeny books locked up in the glass cabinet in the library. These were books of moral instruction which the rather pious owners read to the servants.
- Rare stuffed birds in cases along the Bird Corridor (we wouldn't be allowed to shoot these birds today).

What can you do?

- Have a go at the outdoor scavenger hunt (free at visitor reception).

- Try out one of the walks around the lake or to the church.
- Complete the arduous task of eating an ice-cream from the ice-cream van.

Special events

Previous visitors have found out what lives in the long grass on one of Felbrigg's August family nature hunts. Other events have included a Victorian living history day when you could have a go at butter-making, writing with quill pens – and even laundry work (makes a nice break for parents!).

By the way...

There's free baby food in the restaurant.

A tub designed for modest bathers!

Hatfield Forest

Ancient forest Cycling Fishing Lakes Walks

This rare medieval forest is a lovely place for a day out with plenty of space for picnics, walking the dog and riding bikes. You can even have a game of football on open rides, or plains, which date back to Norman times. You can easily walk around the lakes with a buggy, although some areas are muddy in winter.

What can you see?
- Some very ancient trees.
- Up to 100 fallow deer live in the woods.

What can you do?
- Walk round the lakes, stream and marsh reserve.
- Have a go at fishing in the lake. (Get day tickets at the lakeside.)
- Horse-riding is available to members of the Hatfield Riding Association.
- Cycle routes are available through the forest.

Special events
Include pond dipping, treasure hunts, nature walks and countryside fun days, plus a Father Christmas trail.

By the way...
Keep a close eye on small children and dogs in the grazing areas where cattle roam free – and beware cow-pats. There is a very extensive education programme, and birthday parties can be arranged.

Takeley, nr Bishop's Stortford, Essex CM22 6NE

Signposted off A120 at Takeley. Stansted Airport station 3ml.

Car park £3 (free for NT members).

Houghton Mill

Ancient mill   Walks

Houghton,
nr Huntingdon,
Cambridgeshire
PE17 2AZ
Tel (01480) 301494

In village of Houghton,
signposted off A1123 to
Huntingdon. Huntingdon
station 3$^1/_2$ ml.

Children can dip their hands into trays of wheat and flour and pull on ropes and pulleys at this splendid working flour mill. There are pleasant walks by the River Ouse and through the water meadows. There has been a mill on this spot since 974. The Domesday Survey in 1086 valued the mill at 20 shillings – that's £1!

What can you see?

- All the water wheels, grinding stones, cogs and shafts, making this a dream day out for anyone into discovering how things work. Find out what a damsel or hopper was for.

What can you do?

- Have a go at turning the model millstones and pull on the rope to lift the bags of flour.
- Watch the mill milling every Sunday (when open).

- Follow the trail around Houghton village.
- Buy milled flour to take home.
- If you like the idea of sleeping near running water, there is a small campsite at Houghton Mill run by the Caravan Club.

By the way...

Keep a close eye on children on the riverbank, and watch out for horses on the bridleway.

Ickworth House & Park

Historic house   Garden   Play area   Woods

An eccentric 18th-century house built by an eccentric man – the 4th Earl of Bristol – where there's loads going on for children and families. The main body of the house is circular with corridors curving off to the sides.

There are great gardens with a collection of tree stumps (fashionable in Victorian times) and massive stones brought from the Giant's Causeway in Northern Ireland. The challenging children's play area, cycle route, and trails of all kinds make Ickworth even more attractive for younger family members....

Ickworth, The Rotunda, Horringer, Bury St Edmunds, Suffolk IP29 5QE
Tel (01284) 735270

In Horringer, 3ml SW of Bury St Edmunds on W side of A143. Bury St Edmunds station 3ml. Bus: From Haverhill, Bury St Edmunds or Colchester.

Family ticket: children accompanying two adults admitted at reduced price

Meals on wheels
It was so far from the kitchens to the dining room that servants sometimes cycled along the basement corridors to keep the food from getting cold!

What can you see?
- The screens by the fireplace to stop the heat from the fire melting ladies' make-up.
- The family's collection of silver fish, fans, miniatures and all kinds of intriguing objects....

continued...

Ickworth continued...

What can you do?
- Play football and other sports in the special area for ball games.
- Try out the challenging play area.
- Spot some of the deer from the deer hide.
- Try on replica Georgian clothes.
- Handle all kinds of historic objects on request.
- Follow the tree, garden texture or mystery photo trails.
- Take your bikes and follow the family cycle route through the grounds.

Special events
Older children will be fascinated by the 'Putting to bed' and 'House opening' tours at the start and end of winter. There are plenty of other special events too.

Oxburgh Hall

Historic house   Garden   Woods

This 15th-century manor house has a moat and battlements as on a castle. The same Catholic family, the Bedingfelds, has lived at Oxburgh for 500 years, and their history reminds us of what Roman Catholics had to put up with after the Reformation. Children are fascinated by the priest hole, where priests, in fear of their lives, hid whenever soldiers turned up.

Oxborough, King's Lynn, Norfolk PE33 9PS
Tel (01366) 328258

In Oxborough, 7ml SW of Swaffham on S side of Stoke Ferry road. Downham Market station 10ml.

What can you see?
- Embroideries made by Mary Queen of Scots when she was Elizabeth I's prisoner.
- An 18th-century maternity dress.
- Civil War weapons and armour in the gatehouse.

What can you do?
- Play hide-and-seek in the woodlands and surrounding fields.
- Check out where the drawbridge used to be.
- Look for the priest hole.

Did you know?
A ha-ha is a ditch dug on the edge of a field to keep cows and sheep out. Can you think why they didn't just grow a hedge?

Special events
Most years there are events such as Easter egg trails, competitions and children's extravaganzas.

By the way
Take extra care near the moat.

North Norfolk Coast

The North Norfolk coast is one of the most unspoilt and evocative places in Britain with its wide expanses of countryside under huge skies. It is particularly important for birdlife.

Top: The Arctic tern is a common sight on the Norfolk coast.
Above: Children get creative in the sand at the Brancaster Millennium Activity Centre.
Opposite: Morston Marshes.

Blakeney Point

A long spit of sand and shingle between Wells and Sheringham. Access by boat from Blakeney or Morston, both off A149. Tel (01263) 740480

Children love the boat trip out across the estuary to the beautiful and remote Blakeney Point. Boats get close to the basking seals. The spit also has colonies of terns, ringed plovers and oyster-catchers – over 260 species of bird have been spotted there. You can also walk from Cley, but it's a 3-mile trudge across shingle.

Morston and Stiffkey Marshes

A large strip of marshland on the coast between Wells and Blakeney. Access from A149. Pay and display car park

Catch crabs and jump across the creeks of this maze of mudflats and saltings opposite Blakeney Point. Older children will enjoy a walk across the marshes between Morston and Stiffkey – and keep an eye out for the Brent geese and shelduck which winter here. Look out for samphire, sea lavender and butterflies.

Sheringham Park

A landscaped park 5ml NE of Holt, 2ml SW of Sheringham. Charge for car parking

See the sea from the viewing tower and enjoy the woods of this beautiful parkland. The landscape is one of the best examples of the design work of the famous Humphry Repton. There are some great waymarked walks, one of which ends at an old steam railway at the North Norfolk railway station.

West Runton

A stretch of heathland and woods along Holt–Cromer ridge off A149, 1ml S of West Runton station. Footpaths from Britons and Calves Well lanes

Children will enjoy a romp around the rectangular earthbank, known locally as the Roman Camp, which includes the highest point in Norfolk. Watch out for the adders and slow worms, and birds such as green wood-peckers and yellow hammers.

Brancaster

Four miles of saltmarsh, mud flats. Sandy beaches and high sand dunes

An outing to Scolt Head Island makes a great day out (boats and tide permitting). Hire a boat from Brancaster Staithe

along the creeks, and enjoy the remoteness of this sandy island, with its huge dunes and beach onto the wild North Sea.

Brancaster Millennium Activity Centre

Tel (01485) 210719

This centre has recently opened, and offers all kinds of exciting environmental courses and outdoor pursuits for schools, from Key Stage 2 to A level. Situated in a prime spot at the head of a creek with marsh views, the centre practises what is preaches: it draws heat from the mud flats via a heat pump, and uses wind and solar power. The centre also runs residential family fun weeks from August 2000. Contact the number above for details.

Tattershall Castle

Castle Grounds

Tattershall, Lincoln
LN4 4LR
Tel (01526) 342543

On S side of A153,
15ml NE of Sleaford.
Ruskington station 10ml.
Bus: Brylaine
Boston–Woodhall Spa.

Family ticket: children
accompanied by an adult
free in July and August

A huge red-bricked medieval tower with enormous Gothic fireplaces, tapestries and walls as thick as a room. The castle, which has a double moat, was used for entertaining important guests and keeping out unwanted ones.

Did you know...
The spiral stone staircases were cleverly built so that a defending soldier standing on the stairs could fight easily with his right hand – it was much harder for the attacker below, forced to use his left.

What can you see?
- The dungeons where prisoners whiled away long hours.
- The original, not too sanitary, lavatories.

What can you do?
- Dare to enter the eerie medieval dungeons.
- Imagine you're a soldier keeping watch.

Special events
There are often children's activity days and living history weekends.

Wicken Fen

Nature reserve   Cottage   Visitor centre   Walks

You feel that you are in the middle of a very ancient and special place at Wicken Fen, the oldest nature reserve in Britain, with its hubbub of natural activity. Walk along the lush green paths or on the boardwalk (fine for pushchairs), and visit the hides.

Lode Lane, Wicken, Ely,
Cambridgeshire,
CB7 5XP
Tel (01353) 720274

S of A1123, 3ml W of
Soham (A142),
17ml NE of Cambridge.
Ely station 9ml.

What can you see?

- Butterflies, birds, bugs, mammals, reptiles ... the list is endless. There are literally thousands of species of insect and rare plants (fen violet, milk parsley, orchids).
- In summer marsh harriers come to nest, and there are splendid roosts of hen harriers in winter.
- Fen Cottage, a typical worker's dwelling of the area, built from products of the Fen.

What can you do?

- Enjoy the spectacular views from Tower Hide. Don't forget your binoculars (also for hire) – and wear wellies!
- Get your hands on the feely table at the visitor centre.
- Go on, in ascending order of energy and age of children: the $3/4$-mile boardwalk trail; the $2^1/_4$-mile nature trail; the new adventurer's trail ($2^3/_4$ miles). They all have trail guides, and you really learn a lot about the Fen.

Special events

Mini-beast Mayhem and Animal Magic are just two of the imaginatively named children's events.

Wimpole Home Farm

Farm   Adventure playground   Park

Arrington, nr Royston,
Cambridgshire SG8 0BW
Tel (01223) 207257

8ml SW of Cambridge,
6ml N of Royston.
Cambridge station 8ml.

Wimpole is a working farm, home to all types of rare breeds of animals which children can look at, touch and feed. There's a great adventure playground and behind neighbouring Wimpole Hall is a huge park with woods and footpaths to explore. The farm was built in 1794 for the 3rd Earl of Hardwicke who was a great agricultural innovator.

What can you see?
There is so much going on for families, it is as if the farm was designed with children in mind.
- See rare breeds of farm animals such as the enormous working shire-horses, Longhorn and Dexter cattle, chickens, goats, pigs....
- There is also a corner for younger children with smaller animals, such as rabbits and guinea pigs.

New-fangled farming
Wimpole was one of the first places to try out new farming methods such as threshing machines, which were thought to be very modern at the time.

A Jacob sheep.

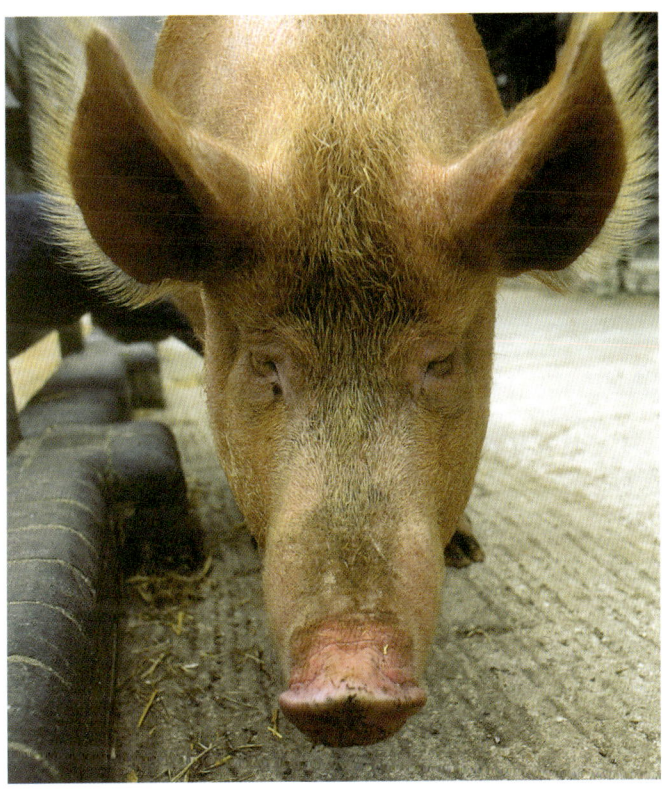

A Tamworth pig.

What can you do?

- Have a go on the red pedal tractors at the farm playground, take a ride on the cart pulled by the shire-horses, give a rabbit a cuddle, feed the goats....
- Just watch the notice boards for seasonal activities that take place throughout the day.

Special events

Events are held all through the year, and include lambing weekends, children's fun days and Meet Father Christmas. Birthday parties for groups of up to 20 children can be held at the farm. Book on 01223 208987.

By the way...

Please don't bring your own tasty treats for the farm animals. Animal feed can be bought from the ticket office.

East

Woolsthorpe Manor

Historic house Discovery centre

23 Newton Way,
Woolsthorpe-by-
Colsterworth, nr
Grantham, Lincolnshire
NG33 5NR
Tel (01476) 860338

7ml S of Grantham,
$1/_2$ ml NW of Colsterworth,
1ml W of A1. Grantham
station 7ml. Bus: Road
Car 606–8 Grantham–
South Witham.

Family ticket

You can see the actual spot where the apple fell in the orchard at Woolsthorpe, and helped Isaac Newton to discover that rather important force – gravity. There is even a descendant of the apple tree growing in the garden. Woolsthorpe is a fairly humble 17th-century manor house, but the fact that it is the site of one of the world's most important discoveries gives it a very special atmosphere.

Irritating Isaac
Newton may have been a genius (a *Sunday Times* survey rated him as 'The man of the millennium'), but he was also a very cross and cantankerous man. He was always fighting with royal astronomers, and had an argument with Leibniz about calculus that lasted 15 years!

What can you see?
- A big display telling the story of the discovery of gravity.
- The descendant of the famous apple tree, and goats, in the orchard.
- An edition of Newton's *Principia*, first published in 1687.
- All kinds of Newton gadgets on sale in the shop.

What can you do?
The new Discovery Centre is brilliant for older children. They can have a go at splitting light with a prism, looking through telescopes (does Galileo's or Newton's work best?), playing with pendulums, and more.

By the way...
The tearoom is only open at weekends.

East

Baddesley Clinton

Historic house   Garden   Lake

Be time-travellers at this exciting house, which in Elizabethan times was riddled with secret hiding places for the hounded Catholic Ferrers family and their friends. You can stretch your legs on one of many walks and trails in the grounds.

Rising Lane, Baddesley Clinton Village, Knowle, Solihull, Warwickshire B93 0DQ
Tel (01564) 783294

$3/_4$ ml W of A4141 on the Warwick–Birmingham road. Lapworth station 2ml; Birmingham International station 9ml.

Family ticket

In a hole

When Protestant Elizabeth I was on the throne the house became a refuge for Catholic priests on the run. In 1591 the priest's hole in the drains saved nine Catholics who stood knee deep in water while the Queen's soldiers searched the house for four hours.

What can you see?

- Coats of arms belonging to the Ferrers family in the 16th-century stained glass.
- Children will be intrigued by the bloodstain from a murder committed here in 1483 – look carefully near the library fireplace. Listen out for ghostly whispering too....
- A 16th-century garderobe (lavatory) leading to one of the secret hiding places.

What can you do?

- The stewards will help inquisitive children find the other two priest's holes.
- Take a trek in the grounds with the children's discovery trail.

Special events

Bug hunts, the Big Breakfast walk and Easter egg trails are typical Baddesley events. For more of the same, check what's on before you leave.

By the way...

Please take care around unfenced water. You don't want anyone tumbling into the moat.

Berrington Hall

Historic house   Garden   Park

Nr Leominster,
Herefordshire HR6 ODW
Tel (01568) 615721

3ml N of Leominster;
7ml S of Ludlow on
W side of A49.
Leominster station 4ml.
Bus: First Midland
Red/Go Whittle 192/292.

Family ticket

There are plenty of things children will enjoy inside 18th-century Berrington Hall, but they'll probably want to be outside stroking the two rare breed sheep who live in the play area, and whizzing through the willow tunnel. The beautiful Capability Brown parkland is a great place for a run-around too.

What can you see?

- Travel through history via the Georgian tiled dairy, Victorian laundry and Edwardian nursery.
- Say 'hello' to Shorn and Hamish, rare breed North Ronaldsay sheep from the Orkney Islands. They live in the walled garden where there are also lovely old apple trees.

- Play 'I spy' with a little help from the garden quiz sheet. Keep your eyes peeled for a fairy (yes really), a sundial and a scarecrow.

What can you do?

- It's quite a zoo in Berrington Hall – the children's quiz will point you to ostriches, dragons and all kinds of other beasts hiding here.
- Don't lose your bearings if you try the orienteering course.
- Children are welcome to run through the living willow tunnel and climb up onto H.M.S. *Sandwich* in the play area.
- Fill up on a Trusty tea-time treat afterwards.

Special events

Hunt out those ugly bugs and Easter eggs in just two of Berrington's family events.

By the way...

Why not visit haunted Croft Castle, just 3 miles away?

Canons Ashby House

Historic house Garden Parkland

Visitors enjoy the intimate atmosphere of this delightful Elizabethan manor house. The entertaining stewards, and a great new tearoom, make this a most enjoyable family day out. There is a paddock for children to run around in and a 30-hectare (70-acre) park to explore.

What can you see?

- Look heavenwards and count the number of animals on a Jacobean ceiling, with the aid of the children's discovery trail sheet. How many coats of arms with a red hand can you find?

- Look out for the brown and white Jacob sheep which are coming to the paddock shortly. The Dryden family used to keep them here centuries ago.

What can you do?

- The old gardener's cottage is being turned into a new tearoom with outdoor seating and a grassy area for little ones to run around.
- Try the circular 2-mile walk which starts at the church (where you can buy a leaflet). Should any members of the family tire, you can easily cut back.

Canons Ashby,
Daventry,
Northamptonshire
NN11 3SD
Tel (01327) 860044

From M40 at Banbury take A422 and then B4525. After 3ml turn left onto unclassified road at NT sign to property. Banbury station 10ml.
Bus: Occasional Sunday services from Northampton.

Family ticket

Calke Abbey

Historic house Playground Park Walks

Ticknall, Derby,
Derbyshire
DE73 1LE
Tel (01332) 863822

10ml S of Derby,
on A514. Access
from M42/A42 jct 13.
Derby station 10ml.
Bus: Derby Integrated
69B from Swadlincote.

Family ticket

Calke Abbey must rank as one of the Trust's most child-friendly
and fun properties. The nature trails are some of the most
imaginative – you can identify the different deer from their
droppings and even find out about talking trees and tree elves.

Despite its name, Calke Abbey is not a monastic ruin, but
a baroque mansion stuffed full of strange objects which will have
children's eyes out on stalks. The eccentric family who lived here
never threw anything away: the state bed, brought here 250 years
ago, was never even unpacked!

Sir Vauncey Harpur Crewe kept his room in a bit of a mess!

Invisible servants

The owners wanted to see their servants as little as possible so built lots of secret corridors for them to use. If they did bump into the family, the servant had to face the wall to pretend to be invisible! There are even tunnels outside – to the stables and to the gardens. You can venture down them and practise your echoes.

Hunting for eggs at Calke.

What can you see?

- An alligator's skull with massive teeth in a cabinet full to bursting – all at child's eye level.
- Collections of stones, shells, cannonballs – definitely the work of an oddball!
- Pheasants in the aviary and newts in the many ponds.

What can you do?

- Find the secret walled garden hidden behind a rough shrubby area.
- See how many people can fit inside the hollow tree.
- Climb on the big cedar tree.
- Do the backpack trail, complete with child-sized binoculars and bug boxes (planned for 2001).

Special events

Face painting, Easter egg hunts and arts and crafts figure among the events at Calke.

By the way...

As Calke is so popular, there may be delays in entry on bank holidays. It is closed Thursdays and Fridays.

Carding Mill Valley

Countryside　Walks

Chalet Pavilion, Carding
Mill Valley, Church
Stretton, Shropshire
SY6 6JG
(01694) 722631

15ml S of Shrewsbury,
W of Church Stretton
valley and A49.
Church Stretton station
1ml. Bus: Shropshire Link
435.

Free entry

Carding Mill Valley is the ideal spot for a family outing in the fresh air. Cycle along the bridlepaths with a picnic on a sunny day, or tramp about in your wellies – and enjoy it!

Be kind to the Long Mynd
Please stick to the paths. Feet, hooves and tyres are wearing away precious heather cover and if this disappears so will the Mynd's birds, plants and insects.

What can you see?
- Breathtaking views over Shropshire and Cheshire.
- Grazing sheep (and lambs in the spring), birds and insects around the valley's streams and bogs.

What can you do?
- Find out more at the information centre in the Chalet Pavilion (loos, restaurant and shop here too). Go green – leave your car and take the shuttle into the heart of the Long Mynd.
- Ask for a map and compass for a bit of orienteering over the heath.
- Borrow the pond-dipping nets – occasionally education centre equipment can be lent out.

Special events
There are lots of events at Carding Mill Valley such as family fun days and storytelling. You should be able to check out future activities on a new website (ring for details).

By the way...
Not far from here are the ancient woods and entrancing views of Wenlock Edge. Park at Wilderhope Manor where information boards show waymarked circular walks.

Charlecote Park

Historic house Walks Park

There are many enchanting things about Charlecote Park but the most fascinating has to be the early 19th-century service rooms (including kitchen, laundry and brew-house) kitted out with original equipment. Families will also enjoy the play area, red and fallow deer and Jacob sheep in the park, and a maze with carved wooden deer.

A bit of history

The Lucy family have lived at Charlecote for at least 700 years. Queen Elizabeth I visited them in 1572 and Shakespeare is said to have poached their deer in the park.

What can you see?

- The 19th-century 'below stairs' rooms. Imagine how tough life was for servants.
- The Lucy family fish symbol around the house.
- An intriguing collection of vehicles in the carriage-houses, including several 'phaetons' – the sports car of the 18th century. Spot those fish again on the Lucys' Victorian travelling coach.

What can you do?

- Buy a children's guide and go round the house in the role of a hopeful servant applying for work in 1835.
- Watch the video in the room above the carriage-house and hear Mary Elizabeth Lucy tell the story of 19th-century Charlecote.
- Enjoy a picnic in the splendid deer park landscaped by 'Capability' Brown.

Special events

Charlecote Park caters very well for fun-loving families with treasure hunts, ghostly storytelling at Hallowe'en and much more

Warwick,
Warwickshire
CV35 9ER
Tel (01789) 470277

1ml W of Wellesbourne;
15ml E of Stratford-upon-Avon; 6ml S of Warwick on N side of B4086.
Stratford-upon-Avon station 5$\frac{1}{2}$ ml.
Bus: Stagecoach Midland Red 18, X18.

Family ticket

Chedworth Roman Villa

Roman villa   Museum

Yanworth, nr Cheltenham, Gloucestershire GL54 3LJ
Tel (01242) 890256

3ml NW of Fossebridge on Cirencester–Northleach road (A429). Cheltenham Spa station 9ml.

Family ticket

Step back into the 4th century with a trip to the National Trust's oldest country house! The ruins of an enormous, wealthy villa lie in a beautiful wooded valley in the heart of the Cotswolds. More of the house is uncovered than almost any other Roman site in Britain.

What can you see?

- Amazing mosaics (still in the very place where they were made). Not one, but two Roman bath-houses.
- A water shrine with the spring still running into it.
- Some fine bits of Roman central heating (hypocaust).
- And, of course, the villa lavatory or latrine!
- There are also many fascinating objects in the site museum.

What can you do?

- Watch the excellent introductory video.
- Then take your very own guided tour. On the CD audio tour, two cheeky Roman children tell you about their home in its heyday.
- For grown-ups, there is a tour provided by actor Andrew Sachs.
- On some days, mostly in the school holidays, there is an activity tent for budding archaeologists.
- Take the site trail.

Special events

There is a busy programme of living history and archaeological digs throughout the year. During the summer holidays there are children's activity afternoons. In late July there is an annual bat walk.

Clumber Park

Parkland   Garden museum   Cycling   Walks

The Estate Office,
Clumber Park,
Worksop,
Nottinghamshire
S80 3AZ
Tel (01909) 476592

4½ ml SE of Worksop,
1ml from A1/A57, 11ml
from M1 exit 30.
Worksop station 4½ ml.
Bus: Stagecoach E
Midland 136 or 251/2
from Retford and
Hucknall Sundays only.

A charge for cars,
pedestrians free

If you enjoy cycling, Clumber Park is the place for you. Take your own bikes or hire them. Every type of bike under the sun is available: tandems, trailer bikes, buggies at the back for toddlers, children's bikes and kids' seats. Of course, you can also enjoy the grounds on foot – there are wide expanses of parkland, peaceful woods and a superb lake at the centre.

What can you see?
- Squirrels and lots of birds.
- Very ancient trees, some 500 years old.
- The longest greenhouses owned by the NT – fancy a tomato?

What can you do?
- Take your pick between the gentler 5-mile cycle route (young children do manage this) or the 13-mile one for older ones. Finish up with a well-deserved drink in the restaurant.
- Brave the 'feely box' in the conservation centre. You could lay your hands on anything from a stuffed dead badger to a fir cone.
- Make a meal of it and bring your lunch to cook at the barbecue site.

Special events
Spider walks and teddy bears' picnics are typical events. Please call for more details.

Ilam Park

Parkland Woods Walks

Ilam, Ashbourne,
Staffordshire DE6 2AZ
Tel (01335) 350245

4¼ ml NW of Ashbourne.
Bus: Warrington 443,
from Ashbourne.

Entrance free. Pay and
display car park

A beautiful area of open park and woodland on the banks of the River Manifold. It is part of the South Peak Estate, where many farmers earn their living so there are sheep everywhere. Walk down the avenue of trees known as 'Paradise Walk', spot the pepperpot tower and visit the education centre.

What can you see?

- Look out for newts, frogs and water-boatmen in the dew pond.
- Investigate the boil holes on the river.
- Can you find the Saxon battlestone?

What can you do?

- Hear your voice echoing through the tower.
- Snatch a sneaky one at the kissing gates!
- Walk along the rushing river in the steep valley.

Special events

Recent events have included children's theatre shows, nature days and a Trusty treasure trail.

By the way...

A small caravan site is run here by the National Trust, open to Caravan Club and NT members, Easter to October. Wheelchair access is partial.

Kedleston Hall

Historic house   Park   Lake

Enjoy the lovely walks round this 18th-century 'pleasure ground'. There's a lion with a spring gurgling out of his mouth and a fishing room where ladies sat to avoid the sun while they were out by the lake. Kedleston Hall is an 18th-century, neoclassical masterpiece, designed by Robert Adam.

What a nerve!

When Sir Nathaniel Curzon inherited Kedleston in 1758 he had the nearby village moved stone by stone because it got in the way of his grand expansion plans!

What can you see?

- Curious *trompe-l'oeil* paintings.
- Indian objects and furniture in the Eastern Museum.
- You think you know what a 'dressing room' and 'wardrobe' are? They meant quite different things in the 18th century....

What can you do?

- Imagine it's 1777 and take a tour around the Hall with the housekeeper, Mrs Garnett.
- Hunt out the exotic sea creatures in the drawing room and a grand bed decorated with ostrich feathers.
- Have a go at the children's quiz.

Special events

Recent events have included family craft workshops and children's theatre shows.

A portrait of Mrs Garnett, the 18th-century housekeeper, with guidebook in hand, ready to conduct visitors around Kedleston.

Derby, Derbyshire
DE22 5JH
Tel (01332) 842191

5ml NW of Derby, entrance off Kedleston road; signposted from roundabout where A38 crosses A52. Duffield station 3$\frac{1}{2}$ ml; Derby station 5$\frac{1}{2}$ ml Bus: Derby Integrated 69B (Sunday only), Dunn Line 109, Trent R51/2.

Family ticket

Mr Straw's House

Historic house

7 Blyth Grove,
Worksop,
Nottinghamshire
S81 OJG
Tel (01909) 482380

In Worksop follow signs
for Bassetlaw General
Hospital. House
signposted from Blyth
Road (B6045). Car park
opposite the house.
Worksop station $\frac{1}{2}$ ml.

Family ticket

This house is unique. It's an ordinary surburban semi-, but when you cross the threshold you are plunged back into the 1930s. Grandparents particularly enjoy visiting with younger ones so they can reminisce about the past. Children will be amazed to see a 20th-century house with no TV, CD player, fridge or telephone....

A bit nutty...

The Straws were definitely eccentrics. There is a light fitting that has no bulb in it – the original bulb fell into William Straw's meal and he was so annoyed he never replaced it. On the kitchen table you can see where the family kept their knives and forks in the same basket as their hammer and chisel.

What can you see?
- First World War uniform and other costumes.
- Mr Straw was a millionaire but his hairbrush looks as though he didn't have two pennies to rub together!

What can you do?
- Spot the old domestic brand names and designs. Children will easily pick out the Heinz baked beans cans, the design of which has hardly changed.
- There's a jigsaw for children in the Museum Room.

By the way...
There is no access to Mr Straw's House without advance booking.
We are sorry, there isn't room for pushchairs in the house. Please carry babies.

Snowshill Manor

House Garden Collections

Charles Paget Wade was a passionate collector who filled this house with objects from all over the world.

Starting young

Wade began to collect when he was seven. By 1919, he had so many objects that he bought Snowshill Manor to house them all. There was no room for him so he had to live next door!

What can you see?

- Some of the 5,000 objects here: terrifying Samurai warriors lined up ready for battle; Wade's great-great-grandmother's barrel organ; and wobbly bone-shaker bikes in the room of One Hundred Wheels.

What can you do?

- Take a quiz sheet to tour the house.
- Check out the names of other rooms such as Seventh Heaven and Dragon, named by Wade to reflect their contents.
- Take a tour round the organic garden with the children's discovery sheet – there are lots of bugs to see.

Special events

You could find a Neptune treasure hunt, apple day or Easter bunny trail going on at Snowshill. Check for details.

By the way...

It's a 10-minute walk to the house along a bumpy path. A vehicle is available for elderly visitors. Pushchairs are unfortunately not allowed in the house, entry to which is by timed ticket.

Snowshill, nr Broadway, Gloucestershire WR12 7JU
Tel (01386) 852410

2½ ml SW of Broadway, turning off A44 Broadway by-pass into Broadway, and follow signs to Snowshill. Moreton-in-Marsh station 7ml.

Family ticket

Sudbury Hall & the National Trust Museum of Childhood

Sudbury, Ashbourne,
Derbyshire DE6 5HT
Tel (01283) 585305

6ml E of Uttoxeter at jct
of A50 and A515.
Tutbury and Hatton
station 5ml.
Bus: Arriva North
Midlands Stevensons 401
Burton-on-Trent–Uttoxeter.

Family ticket

The Museum of Childhood makes for a fantastic day out – particularly when it's a wet one! There are hands-on activities to interest children of all ages, and the lakeside is a charming spot for picnics and games. Sudbury Hall dates from the late 17th century, with lots of intricate plasterwork and wood carvings. For those wanting a spot of exercise there are badminton racquets and skipping ropes for hire in the grassed-over stableyard.

What can you do?

In the Hall

- Use the 'I-spy' sheet to spot shapes and pictures of grasshoppers, crayfish and other animals.
- Admire one of the grandest staircases in English country houses.

In the Museum

- Younger ones can choose a teddy bear to accompany them around the Museum.
- Make yourself tiny with a

The international African dance troop, Adzido, perform at the Day of Dance festival.

trip down the 'shrinking corridor'.

- Crouch down to look into the mousehole, all decked out as a proper mouse house.
- Press buttons to make toy engines work, and light up the mini-street scenes.
- Have a go at old-fashioned Victorian street games such as cup and ball, jacks, diabolo and hopscotch.
- 'Sweep-sized' children can try a chimney climb.
- In the Book Tower Room there are books to read.
- Fill in the questions in the museum guide.
- You can even be taught Victorian-style lessons such as times tables in the school room!

Special events

Sudbury has all manner of events for children in the holidays, such as pond dipping, mini-beast hunts, art workshops, wildlife crafts and children's theatre. There is occasionally the chance to try on period costume and to have a go at tapestry.

By the way...

If you're keen on seeing the paintings and plasterwork, avoid coming on a dull day as the lighting has to be kept low to preserve them. Children must be accompanied around the Museum.

Children can see how fashion has changed in the Museum. This is George William Henry Vernon, 7th Baron, aged four in 1858.

Central

Acorn Bank

Water-mill Garden Pond

Temple Sowerby,
nr Penrith, Cumbria
CA10 1SP
Tel (017683) 61893

Just N of Temple
Sowerby, 6ml E of
Penrith on A66.
Langwathby station 5 1/2
ml; Penrith station 6ml.
Bus: Stagecoach
Cumberland 100.

Family ticket

If it's tranquillity you're after, Acorn Bank's pretty gardens, orchard, herb garden and partly restored water-mill in the foothills of the Pennines will be perfect. Children will love the rare red squirrels in the woodland and looking for newts in the pond.

The water-mill

Experts are renovating the old mill, last used to grind corn and serve the local gypsum mines. It's taken hours of painstaking work – check on progress in the exhibition.

Wild indigo.

What can you see?

- The orchard in May and feast your eyes on the swathes of cherry blossom.
- Three species of newts (great crested, smooth and palmate) that breed in the pond in the well garden.
- Two hundred kinds of herbs once used for medicines, dyeing and cooking (there's a guide in the shop).

What can you do?

- Find out more about Acorn Bank's past in an exhibition in the water-mill.
- Look out for wildlife such as kingfishers on the circular walk around Crowdundle Beck and rare red squirrels in the woods.

Special events

Recent events at Acorn Bank have included the intriguing Newt Watching. Apple days are held every October.

By the way...

Please take care around deep water. Paths can be slippery in wet weather. Also remember that some plants in the garden are poisonous.

Fell Foot Park

Park   Lake   Boats   Adventure playground

These wonderful gardens on the shores of Lake Windermere, open all year round, are very much a relaxed, family-friendly spot. There is no entry charge and families can treat it like a public park. You can paddle and swim here safely, hire boats to splash about in, or take a ferry to Lakeside Pier. Pleasure boats cruise gracefully up and down the water in the summer holidays.

Newby Bridge, Ulverston, Cumbria LA12 8NN
Tel (015395) 31273

At S end of Lake Windermere on E shore, entrance from A592. Bus: Stagecoach Cumberland 518.

A bit of history
Fell Foot Park was once the garden of a big house which has now been demolished. The National Trust is gradually restoring the landscaped park to its former Victorian glory.

What can you see?
- Prickly monkey puzzles and huge giant redwood trees in the park. Pick up the 'tree discovery trail' leaflet for a buggy-friendly walk.
- Uplifting views of the Lakeland fells to the north.

What can you do?
- Children will get very excited about the magnificent adventure playground here with its special section for children under seven.
- On a hot day, bring a picnic basket, bats and balls and swimming things to spend the whole day here – there's no shortage of things to do.

Events
Lots of family events take place at Fell Foot. Recent excitements have included an Easter egg hunt and medieval weekends with mock battles, archery and historical cooking.

By the way...
Please heed danger warnings and always supervise children when swimming.

Formby

Beach   Woods

Victoria Road, Freshfield,
Formby, Sefton L37 1LJ
Tel (01704) 878591

15ml N of Liverpool; 2ml
W of Formby.
Freshfield station 1ml.
Bus: ABC 161/4/5.

Rare red squirrels and a glorious beach are the star attractions at Formby and, we promise, neither will disappoint. In the woods, the squirrels are brave enough to scamper up close to children and the beach is long, sandy and safe. What more could you ask?

What can you see?

- Playful squirrels chasing each other up and down the tall pine trees.
- On a bright day glimpse the mountains of the Lake District from the viewing platform on the beach. Get there along the solid boardwalk, safe for pushchairs and wheelchairs.
- At low tide children can search for Neolithic elk footprints on the beach – it is a bit like searching for a needle in a haystack, though!

What can you do?

- Keep very still and the squirrels in the nature reserve will let children feed them. Take your own nibbles (or buy peanuts at the kiosk).
- Find out about these rare endangered creatures from the children's booklet available at the kiosk.
- Splash about on the sea-shore but try not to disturb the waders and gulls.

Special events

There are plenty of family-friendly activities going on throughout the year. See the notice-board at the entrance or call for details.

By the way...

There is no café or shop, but as Formby's sand dunes are the perfect spot for sheltered picnics, bring your own goodies. Ice-creams are available from a van.

Gawthorpe Hall

Historic house   Garden   Woods

Take the family for a visit to Gawthorpe Hall and travel back in time. The house was built in the early 1600s by the Shuttleworth family, and restored in the mid-19th century; there are fascinating objects from both periods of history. Stewards are always happy to explain the house and its contents but children will probably be most intrigued by the giant wooden fish lurking in the grounds.

Padiham, nr Burnley,
Lancashire BB12 8UA
Tel (01282) 771004

³/₄ ml E of Padiham,
on N of A671.
Rose Grove station 2ml.
Frequent bus service
from Burnley.

Family ticket

The Pendle witches
Village people in 17th-century Lancashire were very superstitious and old women were often accused of being witches. The owner of Gawthorpe, Richard Shuttleworth, was no exception. He was one of the magistrates who sent the famous Pendle witches to their trial and execution in 1612.

What can you see?
- Textiles, lace and costumes from all over the world.
- If you're lucky, wild swans and a grey heron on the pond.

What can you do?
- Let the children's I-spy sheet lead you to treasures such as the four-poster bed covered in carvings.
- Follow the easy 20-minute Big Fish walk in the woods

to find the wooden fish carved out of a tree.

Special events
During the summer there are events for all ages, including open-air theatre. On occasion, the Victorian basement kitchens are opened to the public and you can meet the 19th-century mistress of Gawthorpe, Lady Blanche Shuttleworth, and her servants. Check for details.

Little Moreton Hall

Historic house Garden

Congleton,
Cheshire CW12 4SD
Tel (01260) 272018

4ml SW of Congleton
on E side of A34.
Kidsgrove station 3ml;
Congleton station 4 1/2 ml.
Bus: First PMT 77.

Family ticket

Children love this crooked house which seems to come straight out of a fairy tale. They can wander around the house and Elizabethan knot garden and let their imaginations go wild. Fans of costume drama will recognise the Hall from its starring role in *Moll Flanders*.

Oi! That's my window!

The Hall has tiny windows because glass was so expensive. When rich Elizabethans travelled they sometimes took their windows with them so they wouldn't be stolen, until a law banned this in 1579!

What can you see?
- Unusual patterns and carvings on the outside of the house. Look in the corner of the courtyard for messages written in the woodwork by Tudor carpenters.
- A cupboard probably used for storing spices, the status food of Elizabethan cooking.
- The garderobe (lavatory). Why do you think it stuck out over the moat...?

What can you do?
- Ask for the free children's quiz to fill in as you explore.
- Hunt in the Guest's Parlour for the sliding panel into the secret room.
- Feed the fish and ducks swimming in the moat and then tuck into Cheshire Cat biscuits in the restaurant.

Special events

Visit at Christmas when the house is decorated in traditional style, or scare yourselves with a spooky evening ghost tour at Hallowe'en.

By the way...

Little Moreton Hall is open from Wednesday to Sunday, and on bank holiday Mondays and Good Friday.

Can you guess who the tiny door was for?

Lyme Park

Historic house   Adventure playground   Garden   Park

Take a day trip from the busy city and enjoy the wide open spaces of Lyme Park. You can still see some of the interiors of the original Tudor mansion and children will love watching Lyme's famous deer.

Disley, Stockport,
Cheshire SK12 2NX
Tel (01663) 762023

6 1/2 ml SE of Stockport;
9ml NW of Buxton.
Disley station 1ml.
Bus: Glossopdale 361,
Trent 198/9.

Family ticket

What can you see?

- Marvel at intricate Grinling Gibbons wood-carvings in the saloon. Gibbons was the greatest master of his art in the 17th century.
- Paintings of 'Lion' and the other Lyme mastiffs. These huge hunting dogs were bred here and given as presents.

What can you do?

- Take a tour with Phyllis who leads the way in the children's guide. She was a child here at the turn of the 20th century.
- See where Darcy emerged from the lake in the BBC production of *Pride and Prejudice* – Lyme took the part of his home, Pemberley.
- Each month you can pick up a different wildlife leaflet.

Special events

There are lots of family events at Lyme from Easter eggstravaganzas to bat walks, teddy bears' picnics to Santa's grotto.

By the way...

A timed ticket system is in place on bank holidays. A free minibus service operates from the admissions hut for families walking and using public transport. Ring in advance for details. There are racks for cycling families.

North West Countryside

The Lake District

The National Trust owns more than a quarter of this spectacular landscape with its towering mountains, beautiful, still lakes, dry-stone walls and tumbling waterfalls. Holidaying families may like to target these particularly family-friendly spots. More information can be obtained on (015394) 35599.

White Moss Common

On A591 from Grasmere or Rydal. Bus: Stagecoach Cumberland 555/556 and 599 to Grasmere information centre

From the White Moss Common car park there are lovely walks through ancient woods and along the shores of Grasmere and Rydal Water. If you're lucky you might glimpse roe deer flitting through the trees and buzzards soaring overhead in search of food.

Aira Force

On Ullswater shore

A cascading waterfall is the highlight of a stunning circular walk from the car park at Aira Force (lavatories and tearoom (not NT) here too). It's an easy, hour-long walk but has lots of steps. When you arrive at one of the stone bridges, look into the spray and you just might see a triple rainbow. A peaceful Victorian glade nearby is ideal for picnics.

Tarn Hows

1ml E of Coniston. Bus: Stagecoach 505/506

There are pushchair-friendly circular walks around this peaceful tarn surrounded with woods and rolling fells. Keep your eyes peeled for kestrels and sparrowhawks and listen out for wood pigeons cooing in the woods. Even on a wintry walk on the fells you'll see the

Below: Sheep and Longhorn cattle below Kirkstone Pass, Ullswater Valley. Opposite: Cycling through the Great Langdales.

tough Herdwick sheep which Beatrix Potter loved so much. Walks start from the main Tarn Hows car park. Lavatories at Coniston car park.

Gondola
From Coniston Pier

You mustn't miss a cruise on this steam-powered yacht which has taken visitors across Coniston Water on and off for 150 years. Sailings start at 11.00am (Saturday 12.05) from March to October. Prices and timetable at the pier.

Sandscale Haws
6ml N of Barrow-in-Furness off A595

There are dramatic views of the Lakes from this delightful nature reserve. It's easy to walk across the wooden boardwalk with a pushchair and beady-eyed children can search for wildlife from sea holly to oyster-catchers. The reserve is home to the rare natterjack toad too, with its distinctive yellow stripe. A special pool has been built near the car park for visitors to hear the toads having a singalong on warm spring evenings! There are plenty of open spaces for picnics and regular children's events. A car park, shop, lavatories and refreshment kiosk are to be found at Sandscale Cottages.

Rufford Old Hall

Historic house   Garden

An entrancing house with 16th-century features, and one which caters well for families; quizzes and trails will keep children well entertained and there are ducks on the canal to feed.

Here comes the bride

The ghost of the mournful Elizabeth Hesketh haunts Rufford. She's waiting for the return of her fiancé, called away from their engagement party to fight the Scots.

What can you see?

- The spectacular Great Hall (Shakespeare may have acted in here) with its intricate carved screen. Visually-impaired visitors are welcome to touch it but not children – sorry!
- Look up at the timber-framed ceiling and the coats of arms of once powerful local families.

What can you do?

- Go around the garden with the ABC trail for younger children or the house discovery sheet for older ones.
- Work out how much smaller people must have been to wear the 16th-century suits of armour – would any of them fit Dad?

Special events

Recent visitors have enjoyed magic days, stroking rescued owls with the Owl Man, Tudor games, dancing and stories.

By the way...

Rufford staff fully understand families' needs – bottle feeding facilities are available and there's an early learning table in the sitting room. During the school holidays pick up a Trusty tuck box of goodies.

Rufford, nr Ormskirk, Lancashire L40 1SG
Tel (01704) 821 254

7ml N of Ormskirk on E side of A59. Rufford station 1/2 ml. (not Sunday); Burscough Bridge 2 1/2 ml. Bus: Little White Bus 3, Blackpool TX54 and 754/8, ABC 347.

Family ticket

What animal does this hedge double as?

Sizergh Castle

Historic house   Garden

Nr Kendal,
Cumbria LA8 8AE
Tel (015395) 60070

3¹/₂ ml SW of Kendal
signposted off A590.
Oxenholme station 3ml;
Kendal station 3¹/₂ ml.
Bus: Stagecoach
Cumberland 555.

Family ticket

You'll enjoy exploring this small castle with its original 14th-century pele tower built to protect the Strickland family from the Scots.

What can you see?

- The 14th-century tower with walls 2 metres (6 feet) thick in places. At the very top is a turret where the garderobes (lavatories) used to be.
- The winding staircase with its sharp turns to the right. This made it difficult for an attacker to wield his sword – try it!
- Beautiful inlaid panelling which has recently returned from the Victoria and Albert Museum.

What can you do?

- Imagine 14th-century women sewing in the window seat of the pele tower.
- Have a go at Trusty's treasure trail in the garden.
- Explore the rock garden – there are waterfalls and pools here and 200 species of ferns.

Special events

Come on a Sunday in the summer holidays and join in family activity days with t-shirt-making, face painting and more. There are always events at Hallowe'en.

By the way...

Sizergh Castle is not open on Friday or Saturday.

Speke Hall

Historic house   Moat   Garden

The Walk,
Liverpool L24 1XD
Tel (0151) 427 7231

On N bank of the Mersey;
1ml off A561 on W side
of Liverpool Airport.
Garston and Hunt's Cross
stations 2ml. Bus: Arriva
North West 25A (Sunday,
summer only), MTL North
80/82/180.

Family ticket

Tudor and Victorian features exist side by side at Speke Hall, just outside Liverpool and so perfect for an afternoon escape from the city. Children can search for the secret hidey-holes and look out for its ghost. They'll also be curious about the Victorian 'below stairs' rooms with bells which summoned maids and footmen to wherever they were needed, and the intriguing 'thunderbox' loo.

Speke's spook

Beware of the ghost who has been known to disappear through the Tapestry Room wall to a secret passageway.

What can you see?

- Sumptuous Tudor carvings and wallpaper by William Morris, the celebrated Arts and Crafts designer.
- The 19th-century 'thunderbox' lavatory. This replaced the rather basic Tudor garderobes once used here. Both designs dropped straight into the moat!
- Adam and Eve, two majestic yew trees which are as old as the house.

What can you do?

- Search for the secret priest's hole. The Norris family and their friends were forced to hide in here when it was against the law to practise Catholicism.
- Imagine being a servant here. The feather dusters and oil lamps are all set up ready for you in the servants' hall....
- Walk through the gardens to the 'Bund', an earth bank, and watch all the activity at Liverpool Airport.

Special events

There are all sorts of summer activities, such as designing your own Tudor bedroom in imaginatively put together 'building days'.

Townend

Historic house   Garden

Townend tells the story of the Brownes, a well-off farming family who lived here from 1626. Their obsessive record-keeping of bills and even shopping lists means a lot is known about them and you can get a good feel of their everyday life through the centuries.

Lights out

In the 17th century the Brownes made their own rather smelly candles with mutton fat (from their Herdwick sheep). Today the house seems very dark.

What can you see?

- A portrait of George Browne, the last owner, aged eight, plus portraits of the family's sheep.
- The wooden carved furniture, some of which was made by George Browne. Look for dates carved into the wood and the Brownes' emblem, a double-headed eagle.
- The round chimneys, characteristic of many of the older Lakeland houses.

What can you do?

- Ask the last George Browne about life at Victorian Townend – he's usually around on a Thursday afternoon.
- Help make an old-style rag rug which is slowly being completed by visitors.
- Use the children's discovery sheet to explore the house.

Special events

Townend doesn't often run large family events, but 'phone for more details of occasional workshops.

By the way...

Townend is not open on Saturdays.

Troutbeck, Windermere, Cumbria LA23 1LB
Tel (015394) 32628

3ml SE of Ambleside at S end of Troutbeck village. Windermere station 3ml. Various buses from surrounding areas to within 1ml.

Family ticket

Beningbrough Hall

Historic house   Playground   Garden

Beningbrough, York,
N Yorkshire YO30 1DD
Tel (01904) 470666

8ml NW of York, 2ml W
of Shipton. York station
8ml. On route 65 of
National Cycle Network.

Family ticket

Put yourself 'in the picture' to look like an 18th-century portrait, with a bit of help from mirrors, masks and a wooden leg of King George I! Beningbrough is a dramatic, early Georgian house with 100 portraits on loan from the National Portrait Gallery.

You can enjoy a picnic or garden games in the newly renovated walled garden. It's a working garden, supplying chemical-free vegetables to the restaurant and flowers to the house.

Lady Chesterfield had a very ornate marble basin in which to wash herself.

What can you see?

- A fully equipped Victorian laundry where you can marvel at how servants kept the family's clothes spotless before the days of washing machines.
- Find out what people did without bathrooms.
- Discover why bedrooms were such busy places in the 18th century.

What can you do?

- Have fun with the family making yourselves look like 18th-century lords or ladies in the Portrait Room.
- Have a climb on the brilliant wooden playground.
- Test yourselves with quiz sheets for children of all ages.

Special events

There's always lots going on, from treasure hunts and garden games to Easter egg hunts and apple activities.

Brimham Rocks

Prehistoric rocks   Moor   Walks

Summerbridge,
Harrogate, N Yorkshire,
HG3 4DW
Tel (01423) 780688

10ml SE of Ripon,
10ml NW of Harrogate.
Bus: Keighley & District
802 Bradford–Ripon
summer only, otherwise
Harrogate & District 24
Harrogate–Pateley
Bridge, alight
Summerbridge 2ml.

This rock has been called 'Druid's writing desk' and 'ET'. What would you call it?

The strange and fantastic formations of Brimham Rocks are great fun to run, hide, walk and explore amongst. These magnificent ancient stones were formed from sand deposited over 350 million years ago. Think up names for each weird rock formation, and enjoy the spectacular views across the surrounding countryside.

What can you see?
- Birds, such as jackdaw, nesting in the rocks.
- Grouse, pheasant, curlew and wren on the moor.
- Hares, rabbit and red deer, if you're lucky.
- Identify plants such as lichen and heather.

What can you do?
- Play hide-and-seek on the rocks.
- Pick bilberries in the summer.

Special events
Recent events have included family discovery walks and open-air children's theatre.

By the way...
The moor is a Site of Special Scientific Interest and a very fragile environment. Please stick to the country code.

Cragside

Historic house Adventure playground Lakes River Woods

Rothbury, Morpeth,
Northumberland
NE65 7PX
Tel (01669) 620333

13ml SW of Alnwick;
15ml NW of Morpeth;
1ml N of Rothbury.
Bus: Arriva Northumbria
416; Postbus from
Newcastle. Alight at
Reivers Well
Gate (³/₄ ml walk).

Family ticket

We can guarantee that you will be amazed by the late 19th-century home of inventor and engineer William Armstrong. He was obsessed with water and what it could do, and there are all sorts of intriguing contraptions in his enormous house and estate. Kids will enjoy tumbling about in the adventure playground and the whole family can go on wonderful walks through the woods.

Water wizard

In 1880 Cragside was the first house in the world to glow with hydro-electric lighting. Water also powered its lifts and central heating. Armstrong even used water to create energy to turn his plant pots so that the whole fruit could ripen in the sun!

What can you see?

- Armstrong made sure his inventions were helpful to the servants too. Can you find any of these gadgets: an early version of the dishwasher, the water-driven spit, the dumb-waiter, the electric gong which the butler rang to warn guests to dress for dinner?
- Imagine lazing happily in the sunken Turkish bath located

in the basement. This is part of a suite of rooms devoted to relaxation – for men only!

- One of the first flushing loos in the Owl Suite – used by the Prince and Princess of Wales when they visited in 1884.
- The enormous fireplace which was Armstrong's favourite spot.

What can you do?

- Search for clues in the house with help from the children's guide.
- Wander off on one of the many walks through the estate. The circular Power Circuit through the Debdon Valley takes visitors around Armstrong's hydraulic and hydro-electric machinery.
- Visit the Armstrong exhibition in the old stable block where you'll discover all you could possibly want to know about Lord Armstrong.
- Get tangled up in Nelly's labyrinth, a tricky maze in the rhododendron bushes.
- Enjoy the swings, slides and tunnels at the playground in Dunkirk car park.

Special events

During the school holidays there are family trails and quizzes. Ring for information on the various events on offer.

North East

Cherryburn

Farmhouse and cottage   River

Station Bank, Mickley,
nr Stocksfield,
Northumberland
NE43 7DB
Tel (01661) 843276

11ml W of Newcastle;
11ml E of Hexham;
1/4 ml N of Mickley Square
(A695). Prudhoe and
Stocksfield stations
1 1/2 ml. Bus: 602
Newcastle to Hexham
(alight Mickley Square).

Cherryburn is a little piece of Northumbrian history. Thomas Bewick, the 18th-century artist, engraver and naturalist, was born in the cottage. Today the friendly farm animals and many attractions make it a marvellous place for the family.

What can you see?

- An exhibition of Bewick's life and work including some of his engravings.
- Demonstrations of wood engraving and hand printing from woodblocks as Bewick used to do it.
- The pigs, lambs and donkeys who live in the cobbled farmyard.

What can you do?

- Bring your own family picnic to enjoy in the garden (there's no café here).
- Take a short walk along the south bank of the River Tyne. The birds and other wildlife in this beautiful stretch of countryside inspired Bewick's work.

Special events

Come on May Day and try your luck in the annual whistling competition or get your feet around maypole dancing. There's usually a competition to find the best dressed May King and Queen as well. Lots of other family events are held throughout the year, including a children's art competition. Send a s.a.e. to the Events Organiser at Cherryburn for details.

East Riddlesden Hall

Historic house   Garden   Maze   Pond

For over a thousand years this part of the Aire Valley has been inhabited by people earning their living from farming and wool. The manor house you can see today was built in the 17th century. There is plenty of interest for families: have a go at the free quiz sheet; solve the Riddlesden riddles in the children's guide; and test your orientation skills in the maze.

Bradford Road, Keighley,
Bradford BD20 5EL
Tel (01535) 607075

In Riddlesden 1ml NE
of Keighley on S side
of Bradford road.
Keighley station 1ml.
Frequent buses from
Bradford station
interchange (662 shuttle).

Family ticket

Spooky stories

A Grey Lady is supposed to lurk over the pond. Legend has it that she was starved to death by her jealous husband, while her lover was bricked up in a wall.

Special events

Recent events have included garden activities for 4- to 9-year-olds, circus skills and the Aire Valley YFC Country Show. There is also a carol concert every Christmas and activities for children on Easter Monday.

What can you see?

- A fascinating 17th-century kitchen.
- A room with the bricked-in window so ladies could avoid seeing the outside lavatory
- Old farm machinery in the medieval barn.

What can you do?

- Feed the ducks in the pond.
- Wander around the impressive Great Barn.
- Get dizzy in the labyrinth!

Fountains Abbey & Studley Royal

Abbey ruins   Park   Garden   Historic house

Fountains, Ripon,
N Yorkshire, HG4 3DY
Tel (01765) 608888

4ml W of Ripon off B6265
to Pateley Bridge,
signposted from A1.
Bus: 802 Bradford–Ripon,
or 145 from Ripon; both
connect to Harrogate
station.

Family ticket

You cannot fail to be impressed by the stunning parkland – with lakes, avenues, cascades and deer – of this World Heritage Site. It is particularly good for families. Investigate the nooks and crannies of the abbey ruins – see where the monks washed, cooked their meals and were allowed to talk.

Walk through the grounds at your leisure, and stop to enjoy the dramatic views or a picnic on your way. All in all, a truly inspiring day out.

What can you see?

- The beautiful medieval abbey ruins towering above you.
- The trough where the monks washed their feet in the abbey cloister (they only had a bath four times a year!). And watch out for bats.
- Ducks and swans amid the classical statues in the water garden.
- Some of the most breathtaking views in the country.

What can you do?

- Create your own mosaic, build a medieval arch, design your own abbey or play a game of monastic draughts.
- Do the giant jigsaw puzzle and play with the metal hoops at Swanley Grange.
- Have a go at the quiz and trail.
- Spot the difference between red, fallow and Manchurian Sika deer.
- Look out for pheasants among the ancient oak and beech trees, and identify their trails.
- See how many people it takes to link arms around the gigantic, gnarled sweet chestnut tree which dates back to 1640.

Special events

There are many family activities at weekends and holidays, such as deer walks, pond dipping and mini-beast searches (including tree bashing!). Floodlit tours of the abbey are given in the evenings.

North East

Farne Islands

Coast   Boat trip   Wildlife

The Farne Islands on the windswept Northumberland coast are a haven for seabirds and seals, and a thrilling place for a family outing. Kids will love the boat trip to get there.

Tel (01665) 721099

2–5ml off the Northumberland coast, opposite Bamburgh. Boats from Seahouses Harbour. Bus: Arriva Northumbria 401/501.

Watch out, birds about!

The birds are well used to children and are usually quite friendly. Take care in late May, June and early July, though, when the terns have a nasty habit of dive-bombing innocent visitors as they protect their young. Bring a hat!

What can you see?

- There are 72,000 pairs of birds living here. Children particularly love the puffins with their waddling walk. You'll also see eider ducks, the fun-sounding kittiwake and four species of tern.
- Shoals of Atlantic grey seals are fun to watch as they lounge contentedly on the rocks.

What can you do?

- The only way to visit the islands is to take a boat on a 3-hour round trip from Seahouses to Staple Island in the morning or Inner Farne in the afternoon. On a breezy day the ride is exhilarating.
- Have a chat with a warden to find out more about the creatures in their care.

By the way...

- If fresh air makes your family hungry, stock up on your own snacks – there are no refreshments on the islands. Lavatories are available on Inner Farne only.
- The boat will not make the journey in bad weather.
- You can take your dog on the boat and leave it with the boatman.

George Stephenson's Birthplace

Historic house   Museum   Garden

George Stephenson, inventor of the famous *Rocket* engine, was born into intense poverty in this house in 1781. Hear about his life from the custodian (often dressed in 18th-century mop cap and pinafore) and marvel at just how many members of the family squashed into their one-room home.

Wylam,
Northumberland
NE41 8BP
Tel (01661) 853457

8ml W of Newcastle;
1½ ml S of A69.
Wylam station ½ ml.
Bus: Go-Northern 684
Newcastle–Ovington.

Stephenson's *Rocket*

George Stephenson designed the *Rocket* in 1829. His steam-powered locomotive was the hands-down winner in a competition to design a train which could travel at just 10 miles an hour!

What can you see?

- The simple furnishings which reflected life for poor families.
- Children will enjoy the idea of the truckle bed where the Stephenson children slept. It had to be kept under their parents' box bed, to save room.

What can you do?

- You can touch some of the everyday objects in the house and children can even clamber onto the beds to discover what it felt like to be a family asleep in one room.
- Imagine the horse-drawn coal trucks trundling up and down the road to the mine where George's father worked.
- After your visit, take a walk along the river or the old wagonway – the house is in a beautiful setting.

By the way...

In good weather tea is served in the garden. There are no lavatories at the house.

Gibside

Garden   River   Walks   Woods

Nr Rowlands Gill,
Burnopfield,
Newcastle upon Tyne,
Gateshead,
NE16 6BG
Tel (01207) 542255

6ml SW of Gateshead,
20ml W of Durham;
entrance on B6314.
Bladon station 5ml.
Bus: Go-Ahead
Gateshead 611;
Go-Northern 745 from
Newcastle.

Family ticket

As far as families are
concerned, this delightful
forest garden means space,
space and more space. There
are streams to paddle in,
woods to explore, and lots of
wildlife to look out for. Gibside
describes itself as 'very, very
children-friendly' and positively
encourages noise, pets and
activity.

What can you see?

- All sorts of wonderful wildlife
  including deer, kingfishers
  and herons – and badgers if
  you're lucky. Plus hundreds
  of rabbits scampering about
  in the grass.

- Gibside is also a major
  conservation area and
  the natural habitat of the
  endangered red squirrel.
- You can't miss the Liberty
  Column built after the
  1745 Jacobite Rebellion –
  it's even taller than Nelson's
  Column.

What can you do?

- Pack a picnic and play
  football and other games
  in the wide open spaces.
- Explore the 16 miles of
  riverside and woodland
  walks. You'll find informative
  leaflets outlining routes in
  the information centre
  adjacent to the shop.
- Your dog is more than
  welcome to enjoy a day
  out at Gibside with you.

Special events

Events are two-a-penny at
Gibside. Children's days
(no extra charge) include
magicians, races and much
more. Check for details.

Hadrian's Wall & Housesteads Fort

Ancient monument   Museum

Children will be absolutely intrigued by the ruins of communal Roman lavatories at Housesteads Fort, one of the best preserved bases along Hadrian's Wall. The whole area is so wild and evocative, it's easy to imagine life for a Roman soldier stationed on these moors 2,000 years ago.

A way with walls

It took Emperor Hadrian's soldiers more than 6 years to finish the wall which they began in AD122. Nowadays, looking after the wall – a World Heritage Site – is a full-time job. Stones in fragile sections are painstakingly replaced with modern mortar, but no new stones are added. The work would never end!

What can you see?

- Ruins of the Roman granaries, barracks, a hospital and some of the first flushing lavatories.
- A model of the fort in its heyday.
- Wonderful views across the surrounding countryside.

What can you do?

- Children can scramble up, walk along the wall and imagine they're Roman soldiers on the look-out for Picts and Scots. Take care not to damage it, though.

By the way...

There's a kiosk for drinks, sandwiches and ice-creams at the fort with some inside seating and picnic tables outside.

Bardon Mill, Hexham, Northumberland
Tel (01434) 344363
(English Heritage)

6ml NE of Haltwhistle, 3ml N of Bardon Mill. Bardon Mill station 3ml. Bus: Stagecoach Cumberland 682 Hadrian's Wall service, summer only.

Hardcastle Crags

Woodland valleys   Walks

Estate Office, Hollin Hall,
Crimsworth Dean,
Hardcastle Crags,
Hebden Bridge,
Calderdale
HX7 7AP
Tel (01422) 844518

At end of Midgehole
Road, 1¹/₂ ml NW of
Hebden Bridge off
the A6033 Keighley road.
Hebden Bridge station
2ml.

Immerse yourself in the tranquillity of these unspoilt valleys, where the peace is disturbed only by the trickling of the streams or the drumming of woodpeckers. Children can paddle in the river and have fun on the stepping stones.

ANTastic!

The northern hairy wood ant is special to the Crags. These reddy brown ants are large and carnivorous. They don't sting but they can cling on with their mini-pincers or, if they're really cross, spray you with formic acid!

What can you do?

- Younger families could tackle the 1¹/₂-mile walk known as the 'Slurring Rock Saunter', and for the more energetic there's the 2-mile 'Crags Constitutional'! Guides are available.
- The new sensory trail has a delightfully abstract approach: find the copper plates showing images such as a hand or an eye. It's then up to you to work out what merits touching or looking at.

Special events

If you like to get up at 4.30am to hear the dawn chorus, this is the place for you. Most years there are also prehistoric survival days for older children, as well as bat walks. Check for details.

Lindisfarne Castle

Historic house   Garden

Holy Island,
Berwick-upon-Tweed,
Northumberland
TD15 2SH
Tel (01289) 389244

On Holy Island, 6ml E
of A1 across causeway.
Berwick-upon-Tweed
station 10ml.
Bus: Arriva
Northumbria 477 from
Berwick-upon-Tweed.

Family ticket

Lindisfarne Castle sits dramatically on a rocky crag on Holy Island looking out over the Northumberland coast. Children will get a thrill from the drive across the causeway and playing soldiers on the wind-buffeted ramparts. You might prefer to visit the charming walled garden designed by Gertrude Jekyll.

An Englishman's home is his castle

Edwin Lutyens turned the original Tudor fort into a comfortable, if rather unusual, home for a friend in 1903. See the arched windows and medieval-style ceilings typical of Lutyens.

What can you see?

- The remains of the workings of the portcullis and worn-out stone steps of the original fort.

What can you do?

- As you look around, try to disentangle the original castle from Lutyens' additions. It's not that easy.
- Stand on the ramparts and pretend to be a soldier scanning the skyline for enemies. Be very careful on a windy day. Don't get blown away!

By the way

There is an NT shop and refreshments on Main Street in Holy Island village.

North Yorkshire Countryside

Some of the gems of England's more rugged landscape are found in North Yorkshire, where the National Trust protects many thousands of hectares of countryside and coastline.

The Yorkshire coast

A group of coastal sites extending 40ml from Saltburn in the north to Filey in the south, centred around Ravenscar. Tel (01723) 870423 (Ravenscar Coastal Centre)

Hayburn Wyke is a delightful little bay with a stream tumbling down to a boulder beach. It is overlooked by the impressive and aptly named Beast Cliff (not NT). At Ravenscar you can follow a geological trail to find out how this beautiful area of crumbling cliffs was formed. There are also guided walks from the coastal centre. For older children happy to do more than stretch their legs, the Cleveland Way follows the clifftops. It has some stunning craggy views – watch out for nesting birds and orchids. The coastline is dotted with the remains of old mines.

Cayton Bay

A bay 3ml south of Scarborough. Access to the beach through woods. Car park is $1/2$ ml away

This broad sandy beach is very popular with families, with good swimming and plenty of rock pools. There are also woods and ponds to explore for the more adventurous.

Below left: The waterfall at Hayburn Wyke.
Below right: Sheep on Buckden Pike, Upper Wharfedale.
Opposite: Upper Wharfedale.

Upper Wharfedale

A large stretch of the Yorkshire Dales, 8ml N of Grassington

Get the wind in your hair and have a great dales day: walk the footpaths of this beautiful landscape, with its dry-stone walls, craggy outcrops and green meadows. With plenty of gates to climb over and sheep to talk to, younger family members can enjoy this too – especially if you take it slowly with the odd snack break.

Malham Tarn Estate

A lake in the North Yorkshire Dales, 6ml NE of Settle, midway between Ribblesdale and Wharfedale

Look out for coot, tufted duck and great crested grebe on this beautiful lake that was the inspiration for *The Water Babies* by Charles Kingsley. It is England's highest freshwater lake and you can only get to it on foot. You could take part in one of the guided walks or try your luck at spotting curlew and lapwing in the wetlands nature reserve.

Nostell Priory

Historic house Grounds Playgrounds

PLEASE NOTE: NOSTELL PRIORY WILL BE
CLOSED IN 2000 AND REOPENS 1 APRIL 2001

Doncaster Road,
Nostell, Wakefield
WF4 1QE
Tel (01924) 863892

6ml SE Wakefield on A638.
Fitzwilliam station 1½ ml.
Bus: Arriva Yorkshire/
Yorkshire Traction/First
Calderdale 485, 497/8.

The grounds of this magnificent 18th-century house have plenty to offer children, from the conveniently located playgrounds to the wide grassy area of the Vista. Inside, the Chippendale furniture – probably the world's best collection – is a feast for antique-loving parents.

A world in miniature
The 18th-century dolls' house, which is 2 metres (6 feet) high, is quite magical. It has a mini-leather dog, an ivory mouse, a dining table laid ready with tiny cutlery and silver plates. Can you work out the difference in the way the figures of the family and the servants were made?

What can you see?
- Pets' graves in the rose garden and sheep in the park.
- Chippendale children's chairs.

What can you do?
- There are two playgrounds for children of different ages. You can watch them play while you enjoy a drink in the tearoom.
- Walk around the lake and feed the ducks. A pleasant walk leads to the secluded summer-house.
- Tea at the tearoom comes in Trusty boxes.

Special events
Each summer there is a country fair with entertainments for all ages. Check for other events.

By the way...
Pushchairs are not allowed in the house, but baby slings can be loaned.

Nunnington Hall

Historic house Garden

Little ones will be fascinated by the Carlisle Collection in the attic of this 17th-century house. It is the result of 40 years' obsession: tiny houses decked out with hundreds of minuscule objects, from titchy musical instruments, to minute screws, files and sandpaper in the carpenter's shop. There's also a river with ducks, and peacocks in the garden.

Nunnington, York,
North Yorkshire
YO62 5UY
Tel (01439) 748283

In Ryedale, 4½ ml SE of Helmsley on A170.
21ml N of York on B1363.
Bus: Yorkshire Coastliner 94; Scarborough & District 128
Scarborough–Helmsley.

Family ticket

Spooky story
People say that there is a ghost of a wicked stepmother in the panelled bedroom. She is supposed to fly through the 400-year-old wooden walls!

Did you know?
The man who first lived on this site was called 'Nonni'– hence the name Nunnington (tun means farm). One of the later inhabitants, Robert Huickes, was doctor to three monarchs: Henry VIII, Edward VI and Elizabeth I.

What can you see?
- A fantastic collection of miniature objects and houses.
- Needlework samplers made by young girls (popular in the 19th century).

What can you do?
- Find out why the tea caddy in the drawing room has a lock on it.

- Look out for the stuffed animal heads and skins collected on expeditions to India and Africa.
- Watch the beautiful peacocks strut their stuff in the riverside walled garden.

Special events
In recent years Nunnington has hosted outdoor family theatre and held family nature days.

Ormesby Hall

Historic house   Model railway   Walks

Ormesby,
Middlesbrough
TS7 9AS
Tel (01642) 324188

3ml SE of Middlesbrough,
W of A171. From the
A19 take the A174 to
the A172 and follow signs.
Marton station 1½ ml
(Sunday only in summer).
Bus: From Middlesbrough.

Family ticket

The two model railways and many holiday activities are the main family attractions at this charming 18th-century Palladian mansion. The horses belonging to the Cleveland Mounted Police (who rent the stable block) are also popular with children.

Funicular fun

Children love pushing the buttons on the 'Friends of Thomas' model railway. There's also a larger-scale railway with life-like models of *Corfe Castle* and *Pilmorr*. Little ones can stand on footstools to ensure they don't miss out on the action.

What can you do?

- Have a go at the children's quiz book with I-spy questions to lead the younger children around the house.
- Enjoy a snack in a Trusty beaker or plate in the café.
- Take the 40-minute circular walk through the woods.

Special events

Every month there's a family day such as a teddy bears' picnic or Trusty's birthday party. In the holidays there is art in the garden and bug walks. Twice a year you can pretend to be a Victorian servant baking, polishing and mangling.

Souter Lighthouse

Historic building   Museum

Souter Lighthouse, with its jaunty red and white stripes, is an exciting place to head for if you're in the area. So long as they are accompanied by adults, children can clamber right up to the top of the lighthouse.

All lit up

Souter Lighthouse was opened in 1871 after dozens of ships had foundered on submerged rocks along this dangerous stretch of coast – it was the first lighthouse to be powered by electricity.

What can you see?

- Victorian machines in the engine room, the heart of the lighthouse.
- At the top of the tower you can look out to sea for miles. Don't get too puffed out – there are 76 steps!
- Watch a 9-minute video about the lighthouse.

What can you do?

- Explore a replica of the cottage where the first keeper Henry Millet lived c. 1900 with his family.
- Send a message in Morse code on the signaller, and decode signalling flags using CCTV.
- Have a picnic and a walk on the sandy NT-owned beaches at Graham's Sands or Marsden Bay.

Special events

Check for details of the annual countryside festival (July). You can also book pirate parties.

By the way...

Unfortunately, access for pushchairs and those with restricted mobility is limited. But cameras at the top can be operated by those below.

Coast Road,
Whitburn,
South Tyneside
SR6 7NH
Tel (0191) 529 3161

2½ ml S of South Shields on A183; 5ml N of Sunderland on A183. East Boldon station 3ml. Bus: Stagecoach Economic E1.

Family ticket

Treasurer's House

Historic house   Garden

Chapter House Street,
York YO1 7JH
Tel (01904) 624247

In centre of York,
by the Minster. York
station ½ ml.

Family ticket

Children will be fascinated to spot the fussy habits of the man who lived in this elegant house at the beginning of the 20th century. Can you believe that Frank Green had studs set into the floor to tell servants where to put the furniture?! And there are bossy signs all over the place.... How many can you find? The house is set in the tranquil Minster Close – great for a rainy day.

Spooky story

A plumber was working in the cellar in the 1950s when he heard a trumpet and saw Roman soldiers coming out of the wall. He was so shocked he fell off his ladder! What's amazing is that the soldiers seemed to have no feet – archaeologists have now found that the Roman road which went though the house was 45cm (18 inches) lower than the new floor.
Weird....

What can you see?

- A model ship made out of bones (left over from meal times!).
- Some really clever paint techniques, of pretend wood and carving.
- Look out for Frisk, Mr Green's favourite dog.

What can you do?

- Find out how they stopped mice climbing up the table legs.
- See how fast your eyes can adapt to the darkness in the King's Room, kept that way to preserve the fabrics.

Washington Old Hall

Historic house

Washington Old Hall, home of the ancestors of George Washington, the first President of the United States of America, sounds as if it's going to be really grand but it's actually one of the NT's smallest houses. Although provision for families is fairly limited, you'll find a very warm welcome from staff and volunteers who are always happy to answer children's questions.

The Avenue, District 4,
Washington Village,
Sunderland NE38 7LE
Tel (0191) 416 6879

Heworth station 4ml;
Newcastle station 7ml.
Bus: Go-Wear 194,
291–5 from Tyne & Wear
Metro Heworth.

Family ticket

Long live America!

This was home to George Washington's ancestors for 430 years. The great man himself didn't live here – he was born in Virginia in 1732, but his name came from this village.

What can you see?

- An imposing bust of the President.
- An exhibition which explains how, by the 1930s, the Hall had gone down in the world, converted into grim tenements.
- Remains of the original medieval house belonging to Washington's ancestors.

What can you do?

- Let the children's quiz sheet take you round the house.
- Visitors are welcome to relax in the Liberty Room and browse through the books – an unusual experience in an NT house where items are usually too fragile to touch.
- On request, and with a member of the staff present, you can touch some of the fine, heavy carved oak furniture.

Special events

Independence Day celebrations take place every year when the Stars and Stripes are flown from the flagpole.

By the way...

The Hall is not open on Thursday, Friday (except Good Friday) or Saturday.

Wallington

Historic house   Adventure playground   Garden   Woodland   Lakes

Cambo, Morpeth,
Northumberland
NE61 4AR
Tel (01670) 774283

12ml W of Morpeth;
6ml NW of Belsay (A696).
Bus: Arriva Northumbria
419 from Morpeth,
508/National Express
from Newcastle.

Family ticket

The outside of the house at Wallington, which was originally built in 1688, is fairly plain. Inside there is exuberant plasterwork that's good enough to eat and some intriguing collections which are bound to interest children. The huge stone griffin heads on the lawn will intrigue everyone (who can invent the best story of how they got there?) and you'll be able to restrain children from climbing all over them by promising a visit to the adventure playground in West Woods.

Revenge beyond the grave

Did you know that King William III died when his horse, White Sorrel, tripped over a mole hill? He had confiscated the high-spirited horse from the owner of Wallington, Sir John Fenwick, who was executed after he had plotted to assassinate the King. Jacobite supporters of a Stuart restoration used to drink a toast to the mole or 'the little gentleman in black velvet' for doing them a favour!

What can you see?

- A stuffed porcupine fish and other oddities in the Cabinet of Curiosities begun by the wife of the 5th Baronet who came to live here in 1791.
- The collection of dolls' houses in the servants' hall. Peep through two keyholes and a mouse hole and you'll see the mouse house.
- Original 19th-century wallpaper designed by William Morris.

What can you do?

- Imagine what life must have been like for the servants who worked in the kitchens here – without any of today's labour-saving devices.
- Children can disappear into their very own room filled with old-fashioned toys and games. No adults allowed!
- Go for a walk in the woods on the estate before a final clamber in the adventure playground. (By the way, ask a steward how the griffin heads got there.)

Special events

Recent visitors have enjoyed Rupert Bear's tea party, a family fun day, Hallowe'en escapades and lots more. Check for future details.

By the way...

Because of the large number of precious objects in the house, babies are particularly welcome to enjoy their visit from the comfort of a front-held sling. These are available for loan at the entry desk.

Chirk Castle

Fortress Garden Parkland

Chirk, Wrexham
LL14 5AF
Tel (01691) 777701

1ml off A5, 1ml N of
Chirk village, 7ml S of
Wrexham; signposted
off A483. Chirk station
1½ ml.

Family ticket

A magnificent medieval castle full of murder, mystery and intrigue. King Edward I built it so he could keep a careful eye on the Welsh. It was also the scene of some fierce fighting between supporters of Charles I and Oliver Cromwell. Go down into the gloomy dungeons where prisoners languished, and climb up the towers (watch out for the 'murder holes' though).

What can you see?

- The dreaded dungeons which are 9 metres (27 feet) underground and have the tiniest windows imaginable.
- 'Murder holes' on the stairs in Adam's Tower (soldiers threw hot oil and stones on unsuspecting enemies below).
- Children's figures in the Long Gallery which show you what was trendy to wear in the 17th century.
- Genuine armour from the Civil War (you can still see the dents from an enemy musket).
- A huge statue of Hercules in the gardens.

What can you do?

- Put your children in the stocks. It is preferred that parents take them home at the end of the day.
- Climb on the cannon.
- Work out the mysterious riddle of the open hand which you can look for on the coats of arms all around the castle.
- A playground is planned for the year 2001.

Special events

As well as Easter egg trails, and scary storytelling in the dungeons, there are Elizabethan open days when you can grind up spices for medicines, and create posies and pomanders (all special events are free).

Colby Woodland Garden

Garden Walks

Amroth, Narberth,
Pembrokeshire
SA67 8PP
Tel (01834) 811885

1½ ml inland from
Amroth, beside
Carmarthen Bay.
Kilgetly station 2½ ml.
Bus: Silcox 350/1
from Tenby.

Family ticket

Kids getting a bit over-excited? Take them to Colby Woodland Garden, a beautiful and peaceful garden from which you can take a gentle stroll down to the sea at the holiday village of Amroth. Staff at Colby have created fun activity packs for children so there's always something for them to do.

What can you see?

- In late May or early June the gorgeous displays of rhodo-dendrons and azaleas.
- Rare trees and birds in the garden and surrounding woodland.

What can you do?

- Buy a safari fun pack – a rucksack full of things for children to do and see in the garden. Choose from packs on mini-beasts, trees and birds or pond dipping which comes with a fishing net.
- There are short quiz sheets which also encourage children to look round carefully.
- Try one of the walks, including a ³/₄-mile walk along a meadow-lined path to Amroth beach.

Special events

Include children's theatre, family fun days and Easter egg hunts.

By the way...

Parts of the garden are extremely steep and may cause problems for pushchairs or wheelchairs. Do take care.

Dinefwr Park

Historic house   Garden   Landscaped park   Walks

Llandeilo,
Carmarthenshire
SA19 6RT
Tel (01558) 823902

On W outskirts of
Llandeilo A40.
Llandeilo station 1ml.

Family ticket

Dinefwr is seriously family-friendly! The main interest has to be the park with deer grazing under the trees, wild white cattle and the Bog Wood, but don't be nervous about all going into the house. Staff and volunteers are more than welcoming and children are allowed to touch many of the objects.

What can you see?

- A stunning ceiling dating from the 1660s.
- Trees in the lovely ancient woodland including vast oaks which have been here for centuries.
- Some very rare water plants such as floating marshwort and greater bladderwort on the banks of the River Tywi.

What can you do?

- Try out the children's house quiz – room stewards are more than happy to help with the questions that fox you.
- Children will enjoy the swampy environment of Teddy's Trail which meanders along the pushchair-friendly boardwalk through Bog Wood to the mill pond (spot hundreds of dragon-flies and damsel-flies here).
- Over the summer, join a Young Environmentalist Day buzzing with activities such as pond dipping and bark-rubbing.

Special events

Dinefwr hosts plenty of imaginative events for families. Recent visitors have joined in with summer 'badger watches' to try to spot these shy animals.

Dolaucothi Gold Mines

Mines   Walks   Museum

Whatever else you do in the Dolaucothi area, don't miss out on the thrilling tour of the mines which were first worked by slaves overseen by their Roman masters 2,000 years ago. Take a walk through the estate (keeping a look-out for a rare red kite) and have a go at gold-panning – if you discover any, it's yours!

Pumsaint, Llanwrda,
Carmarthenshire
SA19 8RR
Tel (01558) 650359

Between Lampeter and
Llanwrda on A482.
Llanwrda station 8ml.
Bus: Thomas Bros 284
from Llandeilo,
Tuesday only.

Family ticket

Clomp, clomp, here comes Ned

Listen out for the ghost of 'Ned', a Victorian miner who took a tumble down an ore-shaft. All that was ever found of him was one boot....

What can you see?

- Tunnels and open site casts left by Roman and then by Victorian miners.
- Pick marks in the rocks made by the slaves.
- A collection of 1930s equipment and an audio-visual exhibition on the mine's history.

What can you do?

- Discover how tough it was to be a miner in the hour-long underground tour of the gloomy mine, lit only by your lamps (there's a mini self-guided tour for under-5s).
- Take a waymarked walk or hire cycles for a ride through the estate.
- Kids can get togged up in a toga, weigh gold and try out other historical activities.

Special events

The whole family can make their own swords and outfits and pretend to be a Roman in the annual living history day.

By the way...

Don't forget strong shoes for the underground tour, which unfortunately is not suitable for those with poor mobility.

Erddig

Historic house   Garden   Park   Woodland walks

Nr Wrexham
LL13 0YT
Tel (01978) 355314

2ml S of Wrexham.
Wrexham Central station
1ml; Wrexham General
station 1½ ml.

Family ticket

Your family will love Erddig, where the owners were so close to their servants that they wrote poems about them! The servants' rooms are an intriguing taste of life 'below stairs' and there are often fun family events to take part in. Well worth a visit.

Did you know?

When the National Trust took over the care of Erddig in 1973, it was a disaster zone. Rain had poured onto the 18th-century state bed and sheep had been exploring in the saloon. Painstaking conservation work restored the bed to the glorious state you see today.

What can you see?

- The Georgian kitchens, forge, stables and more, with assortments of original objects.
- The Yorkes were odd owners of a grand house – they commissioned portraits and took photographs of

One of the servants at Erddig, whose title was the 'spider-brusher'.

their servants and, what's more, wrote poems about them. See these on display in the servants' hall and basement passage.

- The stunning restored bed with its Chinese hangings in the State Bedroom. The bed is now kept in semi-darkness and behind glass (well away from sheep!).
- The 18th-century cylindrical waterfall known as 'cup and saucer' in the park.

What can you do?

- Get your hands on a children's guide to give you the full fascinating story.
- Occasionally 'Victorian' servants work in the house. Contact Erddig for details.
- There are easy family-friendly walks along the river or through the woodland.

Special events

Erddig runs lots of events, from Trusty fancy dress days to kite-making.

Penrhyn Castle

Castle   Adventure playground   Museums   Park   Woodland

Bangor, Gwynedd
LL57 4HN
Tel (01248) 353084

1ml E of Bangor at
Llandegai on A5122.
Bangor station 2ml.
Bus: Arriva Cymru 5/B,
Purple 6/7, D&G 66.

Family ticket

Penrhyn Castle looks like an 11th-century Norman castle but it was actually built between 1820 and 1845 for the wealthy Pennant family. A fake castle is still a castle in our book though, and it's well worth a visit, especially since there is so much going on. A children's audio tour of the castle, smashing adventure playground (where your children will probably want to spend most of their time) and other attractions, such as museums of railways and dolls, will keep everyone happy.

Easy as A B C

Richard Pennant was an 18th-century businessman who made a fortune as the owner of the local slate quarry, the largest in the world. Each year his workers manufactured 136,000 slates for school-children to write on.

What can you see?

- Can you spot two chamber pots hidden in the dining room? They meant the men didn't have to walk to the lavatory after dinner!
- The Victorian servants' quarters, kitchen and larder. From September 2000, these will be set up as if in preparation for the Prince of Wales's visit in 1894. On the menu then was foie gras in aspic and pineapple ice-cream. Very tasty.

What can you do?

- Scare the family by copying the gruesome faces carved into pillars on the Grand Staircase – every pillar is different.
- From September 2000 you can smell goodies being cooked for the Prince's visit and hands-on cooking activities may be on offer – check beforehand.
- Pick up your map and instructions from the shop and try some family orienteering in the beautiful 16-hectare (40-acre) grounds.
- Tumble about in the adventure playground or look for the mock ruined Gothic chapel and pet cemetery.
- If anyone in your family is a train-buff, you must visit the

Railway Museum to see locomotives and trucks used in Penrhyn quarry.

- Visit the new Dolls' Museum with over 500 dolls, and the new Railway Memorabilia and Model Museum, fitted up like an old station waiting room.
- Explore the wonderfully named Bog Garden.
- Get stuck into the interactive exhibition full of countryside facts and figures.

Special events
Every year there are dozens of family events at Penrhyn. Check for details.

By the way...
Pushchairs are unfortunately not allowed in the house, but paths on the estate are very pushchair (and wheelchair) friendly.

Plas Newydd

Historic house Boat trip Garden Museum Walks

Everyone loves a boat trip and it'll be fun boarding the *Snowdon Queen* from Plas Newydd after a visit to this elegant 18th-century house and gardens. Explore the military museum to find a fake leg.

Llanfairpwll, Anglesey
LL61 6DQ
Tel (01248) 714795

2ml SW of Llanfairpwll and A5 on A4080. Llanfairpwll station 1¾ml. Bus: Arriva Cymru 42 from Bangor station.

Family ticket

What can you see?

- The enormous painting by Rex Whistler – can you find Neptune's footsteps?
- An artificial leg made for the 1st Marquess of Anglesey after he lost his leg at the Battle of Waterloo.

The 5th Marquess loved dressing up and taking part in theatricals.

What can you do?

- Let the children's quiz trail lead you around the garden to earn a free treat in the tea-room (family fun days only).
- Take a 40-minute boat trip on the *Snowdon Queen*, from the jetty along the Menai Strait to Britannia Bridge and back.
- Clamber up into the tree-house built for the present Lord Anglesey's children.
- Go for a stroll through the woodland to a tranquil marine walk.

Special events

Plas Newydd holds at least 12 family days a year, all packed with well-entertained families. Join in with seasonal events such as egg rolling, face-painting and treasure hunts.

By the way...

Bottle heating, colouring sheets and Trusty lunch boxes are all on offer for families in the tearoom.

Powis Castle

Historic house   Garden   Museum

Welshpool, Powys
SY21 8RF
Tel (01938) 554338

1ml S of Welshpool.
Welshpool station 1³/₄ ml.
Bus: Arriva North
Midlands D71/D75
to High Street.

Family ticket

Powis is a massive castle, built high on a rocky perch by Welsh princes in the 13th century. It is famous for its 300-year-old yew trees and collection of Indian treasures. Children are catered for excellently with special menus and plenty of quizzes and trails for inside the castle and out.

Tigor talk

The solid gold tiger head, encrusted with precious stones, belonged to Tipu, an Indian ruler who was killed by the British in 1799. Many of his treasures, including the tiger and his slippers ended up here.

What can you see?

● Beautiful Indian paintings and other objects, like the tiger head in the Clive Museum.
● A giant stone foot sculpture in the Wilderness Garden.
● The igloo-shaped ice-house used for storing ice before fridges were invented.

What can you do?

● Discover more about the castle with the children's quiz.

Special events

There are occasional family events such as plays and an annual Easter egg hunt.

By the way...

Unfortunately there is no wheelchair access to the castle, and not recommended for the gardens.

Welsh Countryside

The National Trust for Wales cares for miles of spectacular countryside and coastline and some glorious family beaches. You'll have a good time wherever you go but the following spots are particularly family-friendly. For further information contact the NT office for Wales on (01492) 860123.

The Gower Peninsula

15ml SW of Swansea on B4247. Parking and lavatories at the visitor centre

The 5 miles of superb beach at Rhossili Bay on the very tip of the Gower Peninsula is the place to head for if you've got young children. At low tide they'll be able to see the wooden ribs of the *Helvetia*, shipwrecked in 1887, and you can all get the wind in your hair on a gentle mile-long cliff walk from the visitor centre to the old coastguard look-out.

The Llŷn Peninsula

The dramatic cliffs are home to rare birds such as the chough and peregrine. When you're out and about, look for the posters of sand castle competitions for all the family which take place every year. A 1¹/₂-mile walk takes you to the pretty fishing village of Porthdinllaen with its fabulous family beach. (4ml W of Nefyn off B4417, parking, café and lavatories.) You'll also discover a delightful sandy beach at Porth Oer, known locally as the 'whistling sands'. (2¹/₂ ml NW of Aberdaron off B4327. Parking. Lavatories and café open in season.)

Cardigan Bay

NE of Cardigan off A487. Café, parking and lavatories at both beaches. No dogs on beaches May–September

There are two wonderful family beaches nestling along this spectacular stretch of coastline. Park at the popular Penbryn beach for instant access, or stretch your legs on a ¹/₂-mile walk through the leafy woods of the Hoffnant

Opposite top:
Children explore the rock pools at Stackpole.

Opposite below:
View through the woods on the south side of Barafundle Bay, Stackpole.

Below: Dolphins can be seen off the coast.

valley, said once to have been used by smugglers. Seals and bottle-nosed dolphins can be seen playing in the waves from the sheltered beach at Mwnt.

Pembrokeshire

5ml S of Pembroke off B4319. Café, lavatories and parking at Stackpole Quay and Broadhaven

The coastal Stackpole estate (also easily accessible from the holiday centre of Tenby) includes a bit of everything – family-friendly beaches, lakes, sheltered bays and woods. There are excellent firm paths for pushchairs, including a lakeside walk with hide for a bit of bird-spotting, and a level woodland route. Children will love the magnificent beaches at Barafundle Bay and Broadhaven. The Stackpole for Schools Centre runs outdoor activity holidays for individual children in the summer.

Ardress House

Historic house   Adventure playground   Farm animals

64 Ardress Road,
Portadown, Co Armagh
BT62 1SQ
Tel (028) 3885 1236

5ml from Moy, 3ml from
jct 13 on M1.
Portadown station 7ml.
Bus: Ulsterbus 67 within
$1/_4$ ml.

Family ticket

Children will love feeding the chickens and wandering among the peacocks in Ardress's charming cobbled farmyard. They can then let off steam in the adventure playground. Ardress was originally a 17th-century farmhouse that was gentrified in the 18th century, with lots of smart plasterwork. In the outbuildings you can find old farming equipment which the older generation enjoy.

What can you see?
- Ducks on the duck pond, tethered goats, peahens, peacocks and loads of pigs.
- Potato diggers and butter-making gear.

What can you do?
- Throw seed to the hens.
- Swing your way around the adventure playground.
- Do Trusty's puzzle sheet.

Special events
Most years there are three main events at Ardress: an Apple Blossom Day in May with Punch and Judy and the like; Country Capers in August with obstacle races and children's entertainments; Hallowe'en with ghostly story-telling, fancy dress and spooky lanterns.

The Argory

Historic house   **Adventure playground**   **Walks**

Step back into the life of the 19th-century Irish gentry, in this charming house with its largely untouched, cluttered interiors. While there are a few objects in the house which will intrigue children, they may be far more interested in the adventure playground and environmental sculpture trail.

Moy, Dungannon,
Co Armagh BT71 6NA
Tel (028) 8778 4753

4ml from Moy, 3ml from M1 exit 13 or 14 (signposted). Bus: Ulsterbus 67 stops 2$^1/_2$ ml away at Charlemont.

Family ticket

What can you see?

- Don't be scared of the large mastiff and lurcher in the entrance hall – they won't bite!
- You might be lucky and catch the magnificent organ being played from the barrels at the back rather than from the keys.
- Find Vic the dog's grave.

What can you do?

- Follow the sculpture trail with sculptures which local children helped to make.
- Swing and balance your way around the adventure playground: cross the Burma bridge and trip across the log walk.
- There are some great walks to be explored in the 120 hectares (300 acres) of woodland and parkland beyond the house and garden.

Special events

Loads of activities take place in the summer here: craft fairs, the Famfest day on the Blackwater River, and a family fun day. Punch and Judy, dog-handling demonstrations, hands and clowns make these really great family days out. There's also a living history day in August.

Castle Ward & Strangford Lough

Historic house   Playgrounds   Victorian pastime & wildlife centres

Strangford,
Downpatrick, Co Down
BT30 7LS
Tel (028) 4488 1204

7ml NE of Downpatrick,
1½ ml W of Strangford
village on A25, on
S shore of
Strangford Lough.
Bus: Ulsterbus 16E,
alight Ballycutter
crossroads 1ml.

Family ticket

Take a ride in a tractor trailer, feed the ducks and swans, handle animal skeletons – there is masses to entertain children here. There are two playgrounds and some lovely walks. Children have the chance not only to have a go at the old Victorian games, they can wear appropriate clothes while they're at it. The house is a jigsaw of period styles, set in a beautiful park, running down to the shores of Strangford Lough. Here there is the Wildlife Centre.

Go back in time

Try on Victorian hooped skirts and sailors' outfits at the Victorian pastime centre, and play old-fashioned games such as hobby horses and hoops.

What can you see?
- Old farm machinery in the farmyard.
- Rare Irish Moiled cattle.

What can you do?
- Take a bumpy trip around the grounds on the Castle Ward Cruiser – a 20-seater trailer towed by a tractor (small charge).
- There's a playground for under-10s, and an adventure playground for older children.
- Take food for a barbecue and play ball games on the lawns.

Strangford Lough

This is a huge seawater lake; with over 50 islands, it's one of the most important places for wildlife in Europe. From Castle Ward and Mount Stewart you can watch huge flocks of Pale-bellied Brent Geese coming south. A festival is held every autumn to celebrate their arrival, organised in conjunction with the Wildlife Wetland Trust. There are seals and otters and unusual flowers. 'Strangford' means 'strong fjord', which is not surprising when you realise

Boxing squirrels, extraordinary examples of Victorian taxidermy, in the Morning Room at Castle Ward.

that 300 million cubic metres of water squeezes through 'the Narrows' four times a day. Watch the ferry arching against the current, and sailboats going backwards!

The Wildlife Centre

This is heaven for children with a naturalist bent. There's a touch table where you can handle fossils, shells, birds' wings and skulls. The staff have stuffed a badger and an unfortunate otter which got run over. You can put objects under the microscope for a closer look. Have a go at the big jigsaw puzzles and watch the video about the wildlife.

Special events

You'll be spoilt for choice at these properties. At Castle Ward there are events such as teddy bears' picnics and children's nature rambles. At the Wildlife Centre you might go on a bat walk, moth morning or shore foray. Contact the properties for details.

Crom Estate

Woods   Park   Wetland   Boat hire   Walks

Visitor Centre,
Newtownbutler, Co
Fermanagh BT92 8AP
Tel (028) 6773 8118

3ml W of Newtownbutler,
on J363245, or follow
signs from Lisnaskea.
Bus: Ulsterbus 95
Enniskillen–Clones.

A magical maze of water, peninsulas, islands with views to distant hills, and parkland. It is home to Oscar the pine marten, red squirrels and badgers as well as rare butterflies, birds and plants. There are all kinds of outdoor activities to get up to, making a great day out.

What can you do?

- Wend your way around the islands in a hired boat.
- You can arrange to stay overnight in the mammal hide – and take your chances of spotting Oscar!
- Do the Indiana Jones trail or the Trusty treasure trail.

Rare sights

Crom Estate is one of the NT's most important conservation areas. See if you can spot some of the following:

... in the woodlands
- The purple hair streak butterfly.
- Rare mosses and lichens.
- Wild garlic, goldilocks and violets.

... in the marshy lough
- Great crested grebe, cormorant and curlew.
- Yellow pimpernel, watermint and water horsetail.

Special events

Typical events held in the summer include a small pet competition, plant fairs and garden fêtes. Call for more details.

By the way...

You need good grippy shoes for the walks if the weather is wet. Cottages on the estate are available for holiday lets.

Florence Court

Historic house   Playground   Park   Walks

Once the children have clambered their way around the playground, families can take in the atmosphere of one of Ulster's most important 18th-century houses. There's a lovely area of cobbled courtyards with tearoom and shop, plus a walled garden. The stunning surrounding landscape, with its mountains and forests, makes a special trip to the area worthwhile.

Enniskillen, Co Fermanagh BT92 1DB
Tel (028) 6634 8249

8ml SW of Enniskillen via A4 Sligo road and A32 Swanlinbar road.
Bus: Ulsterbus 192 within 1ml.

Family ticket

What can you see?

- A blacksmith's forge, carpenter's workshop and eel house.
- A hydraulic ram and water-powered saw-mill in the pleasure grounds.
- The famous Florence Court Yew – supposed to be the 'parent' of all Irish yew trees.
- An ice-house used in the days before fridges.

What can you do?

- Swing and snack in the playground and picnic area.
- Younger children can have fun with Trusty's puzzle sheet.
- Walk the 1400-metre ($^3/_4$-mile) path around the grounds (much of it suitable for wheelchairs and pushchairs).
- The forest park nearby has some great walks.

Special events

From Victorian fashion shows

A Japanese print from the collection at Florence Court.

to craft shows and children's fun days, there is plenty going on on summer weekends at Florence Court. Check property for details.

By the way...

Rose Cottage, idyllically situated by the walled garden, is available for holiday lets.

Giant's Causeway

Rock formations   Walks

Bushmills, Co Antrim
BT57 8SU
Tel (028) 2073 1759/
1582 (visitor centre)

On B146 Causeway–
Dunseverick road.
Portrush station 8ml. Bus:
Ulsterbus 138
from Coleraine.

A charge for Moyle
District Council car park
(including NT members)

Children will be intrigued by these weird and wonderful rock formations which look as though they could have been formed by giants throwing rocks at each other! Or were they the home of the giant Finn McCool? There are some wonderful paths to follow along the coastline – let your imagination run wild and see all sorts of shapes in the rocks.

Name that rock!

Is it a boot or is it a duck? You may be able to pick out the Giant's Organ, Giant's Boot and the Harp. But can you make out Finn McCool's granny climbing the cliffs? The rocks are stacks of basalt which were formed when volcanoes erupted a mere 60 million years ago.

What can you see?

- The spot where the Spanish galleon *Girona* sank in 1588 when it was trying to flee back home after the defeat of the Spanish Armada.
- Watch a video history of the Causeway (run by Moyle District Council).

What can you do?

- Press the buttons and look at the models at the visitor centre (also run by Moyle District Council).
- Sit in the Wishing Chair rock and make a wish.

By the way...

The cliffs are a great spot to watch seabirds and other wildlife from, but do be careful....

Mount Stewart

Historic house   Garden   Walks

There are all kinds of oddities here to delight children: find the crocodile and dodos in the gardens, or the life-size white stag that was supposed to carry the Londonderry family to the afterlife. And what is the secret way out of Lady Londonderry's Room? The 18th-century house has charming 'outdoor rooms' which contain all kinds of exotic plants.

Newtownards, Co Down BT22 2AD
Tel (028) 4278 8387/8487

15ml SE of Belfast on A20 Newtownards–Portaferry road, 5ml SE of Newtownards. Bangor station 10ml.

Family ticket

Animal politics

Mount Stewart was the home of the Londonderrys who socialised with top politicos such as Winston Churchill and Ramsay MacDonald. Lady Londonderry made them all members of her elite Ark Club. You can identify their animal representations in the tearoom (Winnie the Warlock was Churchill and Charlie the Cheetah Lord Londonderry).

What can you see?

- Models of a Nazi stormtrooper (donated by Von Ribbentrop, no less), and of James Bond's DB5 Aston Martin complete with ejecting roof.
- A huge and very famous painting of a horse by George Stubbs.
- Find 'Mairi, Mairi quite contrary' sitting in the middle of a pond

continued...

Mount Stewart continued...

surrounded by the words of the rhyme – and, of course, the cockle shells.

- Dinosaurs, dodos and a horse with a monkey on its back.
- Kiwi fruit and banana trees which really do bear fruit (in the autumn).

What can you do?

- Venture down the underground tunnel at the Temple of Winds.
- Picnic by the main gates and enjoy the stunning views over Strangford Lough below.

Special events

The summer jazz concerts are a real favourite with families. They are held on the last Sunday of the month from April to September (please check for details).

By the way...

The staff will obligingly provide dog owners with a special Mount Stewart poop bag.

Springhill & Wellbrook Beetling Mill

Historic house   Museum   Play area   Walks

There is a domestic feel to Springhill which children enjoy. But there's one room which is decidedly uncomfortable – read on to find out why! When they've had enough of the house, the children can romp their way around one of the walks.

Tickling teddies at Springhill.

Plucky Henrietta

A certain Henrietta who lived in the house escaped from a fire by jumping out of a window, only to impale herself on some railings! Poor thing lost a leg – see her ivory walking stick.

What can you see?

- Kentucky rifles and blunderbusses.
- The nursery jam-packed with toys.
- Rare hand-painted wallpaper from 1760.
- The excellent costume museum.

What can you do?

- Go into the Blue Room. Does it feel cold to you? People say it is haunted by Olivia (who loves children by the way). Her children caught smallpox and her husband shot himself – or was it murder? Ask the staff....
- Visit the children's centre and try on copies of clothes from long ago.
- Visit the pretty walled garden and shell house. There's a small play area by the farmyard.

By the way...

Twenty minutes' down the road, Wellbrook Beetling Mill is well worth a visit. Beetling is the final stage in making linen, which you can now have a go at yourself: have fun taking the heads off flax and ripping it through spiky combs. Then try out the spinning wheel (not so easy!) and see the linen cloth being polished with 30 massive noisy hammers. Quite an experience!

20 Springhill Road, Moneymore, Magherafelt, Co Londonderry BT45 7NQ
Tel (01648) 748210

1ml from Moneymore on Moneymore–Coagh road, B18.
Bus: Ulsterbus 110/20 goes from Belfast to Moneymore village, 3/4 ml.

Family ticket

Index

Acorn Bank, Cumbria	108
Anglesey Abbey, Cambridgeshire	75
Ardress House, Co. Armagh	156
The Argory, Co. Armagh	157
Arlington Court, Devon	16
Ashridge Estate, Hertfordshire	45
Avebury, Wiltshire	17
Baddesley Clinton, Warwickshire	93
Basildon Park, Berkshire	46
Bateman's, East Sussex	47
Belton House, Lincolnshire	76
Beningbrough Hall, North Yorkshire	120
Berrington Hall, Herefordshire	94
Blickling Hall, Norfolk	78
Bodiam Castle, East Sussex	48
Bownsea Island, Dorset	18
Box Hill, Surrey	50
Brimham Rocks, North Yorkshire	121
Buckland Abbey, Devon	20
Calke Abbey, Derbyshire	96
Canons Ashby House, Northamptonshire	95
Carding Mill Valley, Shropshire	98
Castle Drogo, Devon	22
Castle Ward, Co. Down	158
Charlecote Park, Warwickshire	99
Chedworth Roman Villa, Gloucestershire	100
Cherryburn, Northumberland	124
Chirk Castle, Wrexham	144
Claremont Landscape Garden, Surrey	52
Claydon House, Buckinghamshire	53
Clumber Park, Nottinghamshire	101
Colby Woodland Garden, Pembrokeshire	145
Corfe Castle, Dorset	24
Cornish Coast	26
Cornish Mines & Engines & Industrial Heritage Centre, Cornwall	28
Cotehele House & Quay, Cornwall	29
Cragside, Northumberland	122
Crom Estate, Co. Fermanagh	160
Dapdune Wharf, Surrey	54
Devil's Dyke, West Sussex	55
Dinefwr Park, Carmarthenshire	146
Dolaucothi Gold Mines, Carmarthenshire	147
Dunster Castle, Somerset	30
Dunwich Heath, Suffolk	79
Dyrham Park, Gloucestershire	31
East Riddlesden Hall, Bradford	125
Erddig, Wrexham	148
Farne Islands, Northumberland	128
Felbrigg Hall, Norfolk	80
Fell Foot Park, Cumbria	109
Finch Foundry, Devon	32
Florence Court, Co. Fermanagh	161
Formby, Liverpool	110
Fountains Abbey, North Yorkshire	126
Gawthorpe Hall, Lancashire	111
George Stephenson's Birthplace, Northumberland	129
Giant's Causeway, Co. Antrim	162
Gibside, Gateshead	130
Glendurgan Garden, Cornwall	33
Greys Court, Oxfordshire	58
Hadrian's Wall, Northumberland	131
Hardcastle Crags, Calderdale	132
Hatfield Forest, Essex	81
Houghton Mill, Cambridgeshire	82
Housesteads Fort, Northumberland	131
Hughenden Manor, Buckinghamshire	59
Ickworth House & Park, Suffolk	83
Ightham Mote, Kent	61
Ilam Park, Staffordshire	102
Kedleston Hall, Derbyshire	103
Killerton, Devon	34
Lacock Abbey, Museum & Village, Wiltshire	35
Lanhydrock, Cornwall	36
Lindisfarne Castle, Northumberland	133
Little Morton Hall, Cheshire	112
Lydford Gorge, Devon	38
Lyme Park, Cheshire	113
Milford Common, Surrey	70
Minsmere Beach, Suffolk	79

Index

Morden Hall Park & Snuff Mill, London   71
Mount Stewart, Co. Down   163
Mr Straw's House, Nottinghamshire   104
Museum of Childhood, Derbyshire   106

Needles Old Battery, Isle of Wight   62
North Norfolk Coast   86
North West Countryside   114
North Yorkshire Countryside   134
Nostell Priory, Wakefield   136
Nunnington Hall, North Yorkshire   137
Nymans Garden, West Sussex   63

Ormesby Hall, Middlesbrough   138
Osterley Park, Middlesex   72
Overbecks, Devon   39
Oxburgh Hall, Norfolk   85

Penrhyn Castle, Gwynedd   150
Petworth House, West Sussex   64
Plas Newydd, Anglesey   152
Polesden Lacey, Surrey   66
Powis Castle, Powys   153

River Wey Navigations, Surrey   54
Rufford Old Hall, Lancashire   116

Sheffield Park Garden, East Sussex   68
Sizergh Castle, Cumbria   117
Snowshill Manor, Gloucestershire   105
Souter Lighthouse, South Tyneside   139
South Foreland Lighthouse, Kent   56
Speke Hall, Liverpool   118
Springhill, Co. Londonderry   165

St Michael's Mount, Cornwall   40
Stourhead, Wiltshire   41
Stowe Landscape Gardens, Buckinghamshire 69
Strangford Lough, Co. Down   158
Studland Beach, Dorset   42
Studley Royal, North Yorkshire   126
Sudbury Hall, Derbyshire   106
Sutton House, London   74

Tattershall Castle, Lincolnshire   88
Townend, Cumbria   119

Treasurer's House, York   140
Trelissick Garden, Cornwall   43
Trerice, Cornwall   44

Wallington, Northumberland   142
Washington Old Hall, Sunderland   141
Wellbrook Beetling Mill, Co. Londonderry 165
Welsh Countryside   154
White Cliffs of Dover, Kent   56
Wicken Fen, Cambridgeshire   89
Wimpole Home Farm, Cambridgeshire   90
Witley Common, Surrey   70
Woolsthorpe Manor, Lincolnshire   92

Photographic credits

NTPL – National Trust Photographic Library
NT – National Trust Regional Libraries and Archives

NT/Andy Darbyshire, front cover (below)
NTPL/Ian Shaw pp. 5, 11, 42, 45, 66, 78, 86
(below), 122, 123
NTPL/David Levenson, Title page, pp. 25 (above),
65 (above), 89, front cover (above)
NTPL/Jennie Woodcock pp. 4, 68
NTPL/Nick Garbutt pp. 6, 113
NTPL/Chris King pp. 8, 74, 106, 155 (above)
NTPL/Michael Caldwell pp. 9, 99, 134 (right), 135
NTPL/Nadia Mackenzie pp. 16, 94
NTPL/David Noton pp. 17, 38
NTPL/Joe Cornish pp. 18, 26, 56, 57, 98, 110,
114, 121, 128, 133, 134 (left), 159, 160
NTPL/Niall Benvie/BBC N.H.U. Picture Library p. 19
NTPL/Chris Gascoigne p. 22
NTPL/Stuart Chorley p.25 (below)
Charlotte Sankey pp. 27, 37, back cover
NTPL/Andreas von Einsiedel pp. 29, 36, 46, 65
(below), 83, 93, 96, 105, 120, 136, 142, 156, 157,
158
NTPL/David Sellman p. 30
NTPL pp. 31, 48, 107, 152
NTPL/Stephen Robson pp. 33, 63, 75, 108
NTPL/Artist:Leonard Rosoman/Foundation for Art
p. 39
NTPL/Nick Meers pp. 43, 58
NTPL/Andrew Besley p. 44
NTPL/Geoffrey Frosh pp. 47, 104
NT pp. 49, 97
NTPL/Jonathan Plant p. 50
NTPL/Andrew Butler pp. 51, 61, 69, 88, 145
NT/Geoff Hamilton p. 52
NT/Peter Ferris p. 54
NTPL/Leo Mason pp. 55, 115
NTPL/Matthew Antrobus pp. 60, 116, 124, 126,
139
NTPL/Martin Trelawny pp. 62, 90, 155 (below)
NTPL/Mark Sebastian Bainbridge p. 72
NTPL/Bill Batten p. 73
NT/T. Cotterill p. 76
NTPL/Paul Wakefield pp. 81, 131
NTPL/Rob Talbot/c.Talbot and Whiteman p. 85
NTPL/Charlie Waite pp. 86 (above), 91
NTPL/Mike Williams pp. 87, 163

NT/A. Trynor p. 101
NTPL/John Hammond pp. 103, 161
NTPL/Rupert Truman pp. 112, 118
NTPL/Alasdair Ogilvie p. 117
NTPL/John Garrett p. 130
NT/Public Affairs Archive p. 147
NTPL/Kim Oliver p. 153
NTPL/Tom Walmsley/BBC N.H.U. Picture Library p. 154
NTPL/Jerry Harpur p. 164
Pacemaker Press p. 165

Stickers
NTPL/Charlie Waite
NTPL/William Osborn/BBC N.H.U. Picture Library
NTPL/Nick Garbutt
NTPL/Roy Fox
NTPL/Steve Day
NTPL/Michael Caldwell
Trusty illustrated by Katrina Munro © National Trust

Wild on wildlife

Mystery property

Fill in the first letters of these animals' names to spell the name of a place in Ireland where you can have a great day out.

C _____ _____ _____ _____

Squirrelling about

Scampy the red squirrel* is very forgetful. He can't remember where he hid his acorns. Can you help him reach them?

* You can see red squirrels at Formby, Gibside, Brownsea Island and some Northern Irish properties.

What do you call...

a **girl** with a frog on her head?

a **boy** with a rabbit up his sleeve?

Out of step

These animals have muddled up their footprints. Can you draw lines to join them up with the right ones?

1   2   3   4

Bird quiz

Colour in these bird silhouettes and then match them with their names – but you have to disentangle them first!

RNWE

WSALWOL

LOW

LUCWER

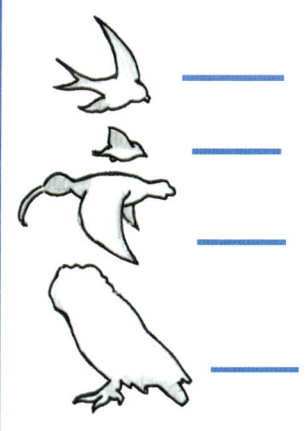

_____

_____

_____

_____

Spooks and smugglers

spooooKcheck

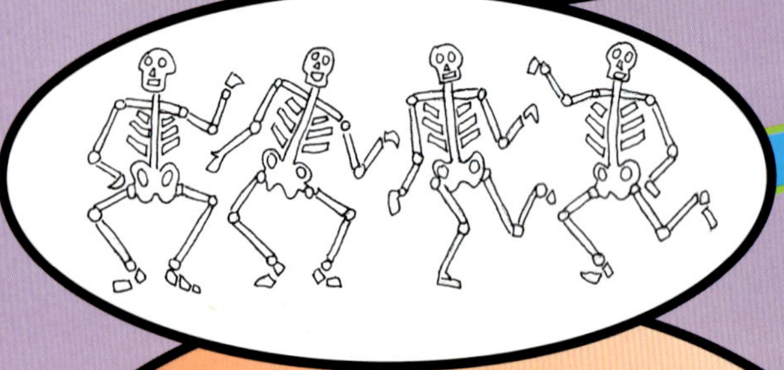

Each time you visit an old house or castle which has a spooky story, colour in one of these skeletons.

You could write in where you heard the story too.

Ghostly giggles

a) What's a ghost's favourite pudding?

b) Why don't skeletons like parties?

c) What do you eat on a haunted beach?

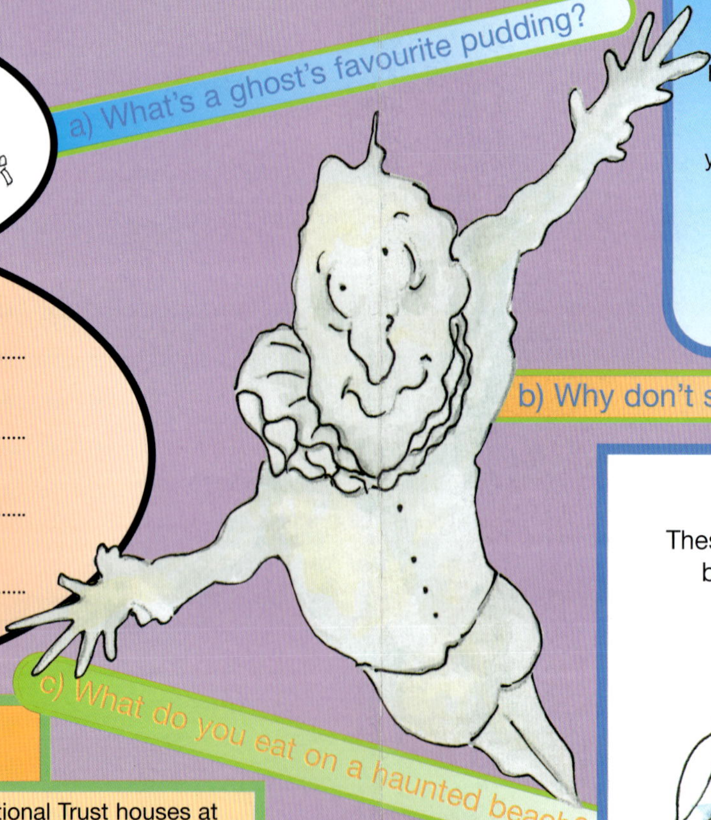

Greet a ghost

You might meet a ghost at a National Trust historic house.

Write in what you think these ghosts are saying.

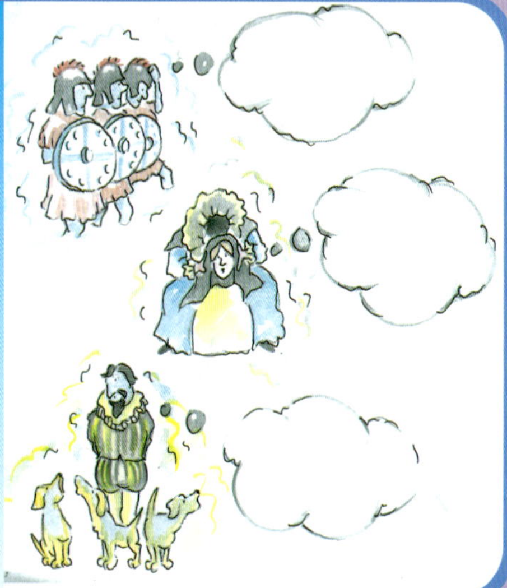

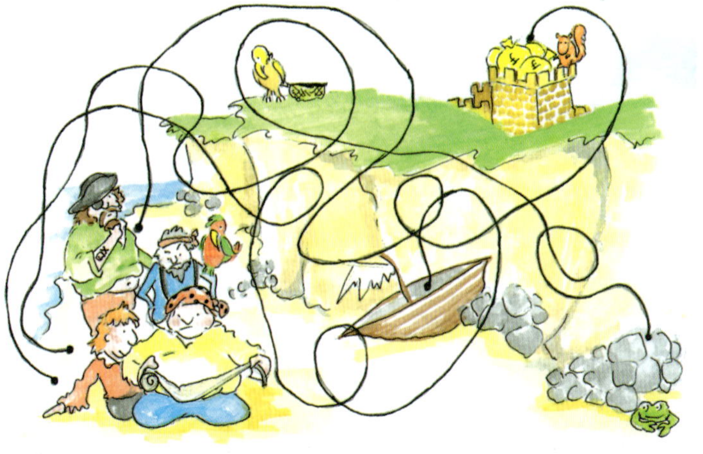

Hallowe'en Hunt

There are all sorts of ghostly goings-on at National Trust houses at Hallowe'en (31 October). Which Hallowe'en object is the odd one out?

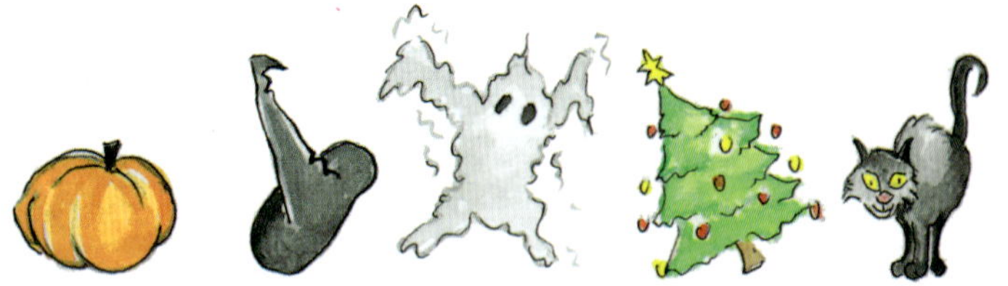

Silly Smugglers

These smugglers can't remember where they left their booty on Brownsea Island. Can you help them?

Bits and bobs about the p▲st

New toys

Join up the dots to reveal the toys that these Victorian children are playing with.

Then colour the picture in.

Luscious lettering

Here are some medieval letters which monks at places such as Fountains Abbey spent hours working on. This was long before printing was invented. Have a go with your initials.

Window on the past

Do you know which of these windows is **medieval**, **17th century**, **Victorian** or **modern**? Write your answers underneath.

   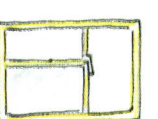

_____ _____ _____ _____

Hat alert!

These three women have all lost their hats. Help them find the right ones. Then write in the boxes the time they lived in. One lived in the **18th century**, one in the **19th century** and one in the **1920s**.

a   b   c

Castle crazy

Secret cipher

Crack the secret code to help this forgotten prisoner escape from Powis Castle.

A ǃ
B @
C £
D $
E %
F ^
G &
H *
I +
J ☜
K ➤
L ➡
M ⟡
N ¶
O ⑥
P Œ
Q "
R „
S ‰
T Ë
U Ø
V ∏
W Å
X Ó
Y
Z ¿

The prisoner's password is ➡%Ø ➡% ⑥∏Ø
It means _____

Why not make up your own passwords using the secret code?

_____
_____
_____

Time travel

This medieval knight is way ahead of his time. What objects shouldn't he have with him?

Soldiers at sea

These soldiers are determined to row to Lindisfarne Castle which has been cut off by the tide. **Draw a line** to show them which route to take.

WORDSEARCH

Can you find all **five** words to do with castles?

C C G Y H D
H R R T J U
A R R O W N
P B O W E G
E H A E L E
L E E R E O
T O W E R N

You're nowt without a
snout

THE NATIONAL TRUST

It's a
frog's life
THE NATIONAL TRUST

COWS
cuddle
THE NATIONAL TRUST

creepy crawlies are
cute

THE NATIONAL TRUST

creepy crawlies are
cute

THE NATIONAL TRUST

I was
spooked

THE NATIONAL TRUST

History is **alive!**
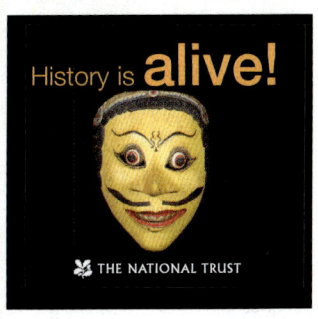
THE NATIONAL TRUST

beautiful things

THE NATIONAL TRUST

Crazy about castles

THE NATIONAL TRUST

I'm a
quizkid

THE NATIONAL TRUST

I'm a
quizkid

THE NATIONAL TRUST

I'm a
quizkid
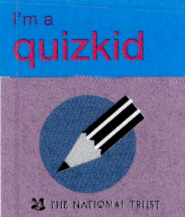
THE NATIONAL TRUST

I'm a
quizkid

THE NATIONAL TRUST

I'm a
quizkid

THE NATIONAL TRUST

We had **fun**

THE NATIONAL TRUST

The National Trust's got it
licked

Trusty the Hedgehog

THE NATIONAL TRUST